Reading Methods in Contemporary Elementary Classrooms

Arne E. Sippola, Ph.D.
Eastern Washington University

KENDALL/HUNT PUBLISHING COMPANY
4050 Westmark Drive   Dubuque, Iowa 52002

Copyright © 1997 by Arne Sippola

ISBN 0-7872-3675-6

All rights reserved. No part of this publication may be reproduced, stored in a retrieval system, or transmitted in any form or by any means, electronic, mechanical, photocopying, recording, or otherwise, without the prior written permission of the copyright owner.

Printed in the United States of America

10 9 8 7 6 5 4 3 2 1

Contents

Chapter One	Basal Approach To Reading	1
Chapter Two	Grouping Practices in Reading Instruction	11
Chapter Three	Holistic Approaches to Reading	21
Chapter Four	Content Area Reading	77
Chapter Five	Special Needs Children	93
Chapter Six	Assessment in Reading	115

Chapter One

Basal Approach to Reading

Directed Reading Activity (DRA)

Step One: *Determining Background*

    A. Elicit experiences from students that may pertain to the content to be read.

    B. Tie the experiences to relevant vocabulary.

Step Two: *Building Vocabulary*

    A. The teacher explains the technical/new terms in the chapter/story by relating them to concepts already possessed by the students.

Step Three: *Prequestioning and Reading*

    A. The teacher asks questions that stimulate and direct student thinking.

    B. Include questions that lead to other questions. Allow students to formulate questions they will answer in their reading.

Step Four: *Review Actively*

    A. At the end of the chapter/story, the class can review by going over the questions formulated in prequestioning.

    B. Disputed answers can be researched by re-reading or by reviewing other references.

Step Five: *Extension*

    A. After reviewing the chapter/story, the students may be involved in further reading or engage in projects related to what they have read.

Directed Reading-Thinking Activity (DR-TA)

Step One: *Preparation Stage*

    A. The students actively review the title of the selection, headings and subheadings, illustrations, and/or the beginning paragraph to make predictions about the content of the selection.

    B. The students make note of their predictions.

    C. Volunteers suggest their predictions which may be recorded on the chalkboard or chart paper.

Step Two: *Silent Reading*

    A. Students read silently until they are able to evaluate their predictions. This might be a single page, several pages, or a whole chapter.

    B. Students may modify their predictions if they find information that runs counter to their first ones.

Step Three: *Discussion*

    A. The students' predictions are reviewed in a group setting. Modifications may be discussed as well.

    B. Questions may be posed by the teacher and/or students that pertain to what has been read.

Step Four: *Rereading*

    A. Specific skills "teachable" within the story are discussed/taught.

    B. Vocabulary words are "taught" at this time. The students and teacher identify particular words that are important and/or problematic.

Step Five: *Follow-up/Extension*

    A. Students are assigned or select particular related activities. One is enough!

A Possible Sequence for a Basal or Literature Lesson

1. **Motivate.** By asking a question or by bringing in some type of stimulus central to the story to be read, motivate the students to read the story.

2. **Build Background Knowledge.** Elicit experiences from the students pertaining to the content to be read. Where necessary, build up background knowledge via discussion, films, filmstrips, videos, pictures, slides, etc.

3. **Teach Vocabulary.** Teach key vocabulary and anticipated "troublemakers" to the children in context. Have the children use their own independent decoding abilities to determine the word. Involve the children in discussing the possible meanings of the new vocabulary words. Abstruse vocabulary may require more concrete teaching (a picture or action). Have the children compose novel sentences using new vocabulary in context.

4. **Predicting.** The children are directed to read the title and examine any pictures that accompany the first segment of the text. The children are encouraged to make predictions about what the story might be about or what might happen in it. Have the children write down their predictions. Have the children discuss their predictions.

5. **Reading.** Have the children read the story silently or, on occasion, have them "buddy read." As they read, the children should confirm or disconfirm their predictions made about the story.

6. **Discussion.** The children and teacher reconvene to discuss predictions and elements of the story. This may also be a time for the teacher to ask relevant questions from all levels about the story.

7. **Extension.** Do *one* fun sort of extension activity. Steal from the manual, other resources, or come up with your own. **Don't do overkill on extension activities!**

I am a dentist. My job is to <u>treat</u> patients by fixing problems with their teeth and helping to keep their teeth healthy. My <u>assistant</u> helps me.

Sometimes a patient comes to me with a toothache. If the tooth is very bad, or <u>rotten</u>, I have to pull it out. My patients don't have to worry about the pain, though. I give them a special <u>gas</u> to breathe. This gas keeps them from feeling any pain.

After I pull a tooth out, the patient's gums might bleed a little bit. My assistant uses some <u>gauze</u> as a bandage to stop the bleeding. Soon the patient is fine, and that rotten <u>bicuspid</u> won't be causing any more pain.

Adapting a Basal Lesson Holistically
To be used with Silver Burdett & Ginn "Dandelion" (Grade 2)

Phonics

SB&G — **The Bridge.** The students will learn the vowel digraphs *aw, au,* & *o* via Teaching Charts and numerous worksheets.

Alternative — Develop your own list of phonic skills you think have high **utility** and **frequency**. Use references such as Richek or Burns, Roe, & Ross for verification of utility. Develop an assessment tool to measure acquisition of high utility/frequency phonic skills. Use "mini-lessons" to teach phonics analytically (holistically).

Motivation/Purpose

SB&G — Remind the students that they will be developing a character chart for the character Dandelion.

Alternative — Tell a short story about a time when you or someone you know didn't act like himself/herself. Ask for students to volunteer any of their own experiences.

Build Background Knowledge

SB&G — Write "Be yourself" on the chalkboard. Pupils share one thing they like about themselves. Pupils write three things they like about themselves on a piece of paper. The teacher reads these aloud while children identify what they wrote about themselves.

Alternative — Already accomplished in **Motivation** section.

Vocabulary

SB&G — Teacher uses Teaching Chart and reads the new vocabulary words to the children. Teacher asks questions about each new word. The children complete vocabulary worksheets.

Alternative — Prepare a short story containing all of the new vocabulary words. Give children enough time to read the short story silently. After completion, do unison reading of the story. Re-read as a group, this time stopping after each sentence containing a target word to discuss meanings and build up vocabulary background as necessary.

Example: **Early one morning a young lion named Dandelion woke up from a deep sleep. He showered and then dressed himself in a <u>magnificent</u> new shirt he had just bought. He also put on a <u>stylish</u> new pair of pants. After that he put on a <u>dapper</u> new hat. He looked truly elegant! That is, except for** one thing: He forgot to comb his mane! His mane was a big mess. Truly <u>unruly</u>!

Later that morning, he <u>poured</u> a cup of cocoa and looked at his list of things to do that day. He saw that he had made a <u>promise</u> to visit a friend that day. He looked up his friend's <u>address</u> in his address book. He knew it would be a fun day.

Predicting

SB&G None is done.

Alternative Have the children skim and scan the illustrations in the story. Have them write down one prediction they have about the story. Have them share their predictions. List the predictions on chart paper, the chalkboard, or on the overhead.

Reading

SB&G The children and teacher participate in *Guided Reading*: Reading a page at a time and asking/answering questions about that one page after all of the children have completed reading.

Alternative Have the children read the whole selection without interruption. (Another alternative is to have the children form "reading buddies" and take turns reading to each other.)

Discussion

SB&G The teacher asks specific questions from the Teacher's Guide. Some questions are open-ended, some are quite convergent.

Alternative Go over the predictions made prior to reading. Discuss accuracy and the "whys."

Extension

SB&G The children complete worksheets, write "thank-you notes," answer more questions, re-read the selection "with expression," dramatize story scenes, write a letter of apology, make an adjective booklet, give an oral weather report (science), create a party invitation, participate in five additional skills lessons and complete many associated worksheets, complete a math extension worksheet, make notes of cloud patterns for several weeks, complete an art sequencing activity, and/or participate in one more lesson on drawing conclusions.

Alternative Do one of the extension activities listed on "Seventy-five Ways to Share a Book," from the other extension activities mentioned in your packet, or any other source. Be creative and *vary* the extension activities.

Round Robin Reading

Definition: The practice of having children, assembled in a circle or semi-circle around the teacher, take turns reading orally.

Quotes from a variety of reading experts:

"At worst, this practice violates the known fact that both oral reading and comprehension are superior when silent reading of a selection precedes oral. The relevant research indicates that this circle reading is probably one of the most effective devices yet discovered for practicing poor reading." (Spache & Spache, 1986, p. 76)

"Round-robin reading, the practice of having pupils take turns reading aloud, is prevalent in many elementary classrooms, especially if teachers are using a traditional or 'back to basics' approach. This process does not achieve communicative purposes and is generally considered a poor educational teaching strategy, especially if it is conducted in a routine stereotypical manner." (Lamb & Arnold, 1988, p. 189)

"Round-robin reading or reading around the circle is often rather meaningless as each child in the group thinks only about what he or she is reading when it is his or her turn to read. A story about round-robin reading concerns Billy, whose teacher asked him to read the next paragraph aloud in the basal reader story that his group had just read silently. Billy read the paragraph aloud flawlessly, and his teacher then asked him to tell the group what the paragraph was about. Billy replied, 'I don't know. I wasn't listening.' Often oral reading of this type can become a rather valueless procedure." (Miller, 1984, p. 95)

Other problems associated with round robin reading:

1. **Causes attention problems in children.**

    Children's thoughts:
    "Well, I've had my turn. Nobody ever gets a second turn. I'll take another look at my new pocketknife."

    "I think I'd better see what's on the next page. By that time it will be my turn."

    "George is really a terrible reader. I wonder what the next story is about. I'll take a peek."

    "Gee, I wish we didn't have to read the same story so many times. I wonder how many more stories are in this book. I'll count them."

2. **Is a pain!**

    Transcript recorded in one classroom:

    "Bluebirds, come up now. John, are you following in your book? Sue, you are not on the right page. Put your finger on the place. Tom, read. Sit up, Jane. Put your

finger on the place. Go to your seat, Dick! I'll talk to you later! Do workbook pages 5-8 at your seats. No talking! Do not work ahead, Sally. That is for tomorrow. You're talking, Joe! What did I say?"

3. **Models poor reading.**

4. **Concentrates on oral, not silent reading.**

5. **Practices word calling vs. comprehension.**

Chapter Two
Grouping Practices in Reading Instruction

Ability Grouping in Reading

Ability grouping involves assigning children to particular reading instructional groups based upon a perceived similar level of achievement in reading. The majority of primary teachers and many intermediate teachers use three reading instruction groups for reading instruction (Anderson, Hiebert, Scott, & Wilkinson, 1985; Stoodt, 1989).

Research by Gamoran (1986 estimates that 80% of American elementary teachers use ability grouping).

History

1. Ability grouping began when teachers in the one room schoolhouse divided her students into groups of those who could read and those who could not (Nevi, 1987).

2. St. Louis Plan (1867)— rapidly promoting groups of bright students through the elementary grades.

3. Santa Barbara Concentric Plan (1860's)—divided students into three ability groups. Each group received instruction at different levels with varying amounts of work required.

4. Tracking also evolved during the latter 1800's. Tracking involved the practice of dividing students into separate classes for high-, average-, and low-achievers. Met a need—place the newly arrived immigrants in the low-ability tracks to supply us with vocational workers.

Why Used?

1. Many administrators and teachers assume that ability grouping promotes overall student achievement and that the academic needs of students will be better met when students learn in groups where similar capabilities and/or prior levels of achievement are shared.

2. It is assumed that less capable students will suffer emotionally and educationally if they were forced to compete with more able peers.

3. It is assumed that students can be placed fairly in ability groups.

4. It is assumed that three groups will better meet the needs of pupils vs. whole-group instruction.

Placement in Groups

Placement criteria varies from teacher to teacher, school to school, district to district. Observational research reveals the following possibilities:

1. Haller and Waterman (1985) found that teachers of grades 4, 5, and 6 did not consider reading ability to be the main consideration in placement. Student behavior, personality attributes, general academic competence, work habits, and even home background were prominent variables in placement.

2. Anderson, et al, (1985) reported that a child's placement in a particular group is frequently determined on the basis of the child's standing the previous year.

3. Spache and Spache (1986) reported that placement was commonly based upon the following (in order of frequency):

    1. The previous book completed
    2. Skills tests
    3. Basal reader tests
    4. Informal reading inventories
    5. Individual needs of students.

4. Riccio* (1985) found that the three most common information sources used in placement were:

    1. Intelligence test scores
    2. Achievement test results
    3. Recommendations from previous teachers.

Instructional Differences

Reviews of relevant research by Unsworth (1984) and Jongsma (1985) showed the following patterns:

1. Instruction for the lower ability occurred at a much slower pace when compared to other students.

2. Teachers spent much more of their instructional time dealing with off-task behavior and discipline problems with lower ability students.

3. Lower ability students read materials that were less interesting and less challenging.

4. Teachers placed more emphasis on oral reading and the teaching of decoding skills with students of lower ability. Additionally, less emphasis was placed upon silent reading and the teaching of comprehension.

5. Teachers spent less time preparing lessons for lower ability students.

*Riccio noted that many school districts had no policies regarding the placement of students in ability groups, and when they did, they were not carefully carried out. This may be one reason why the researchers cited above reported different criteria used in placing students.

Anderson, et al (1985) have written:

> *There are qualitative differences in the experience of children in high and low reading groups that would be expected to place children in low groups at a disadvantage. Children in low groups do relatively more reading aloud and relatively less silent reading. They more often read words without a meaningful context on lists or flash cards, and less often read words in stories. Teachers correct a higher proportion of the oral reading mistakes of children in low groups than children in high groups. When a mistake is corrected, teachers are more likely to furnish a clue about pronunciation and less likely to furnish a clue about meaning for children in low groups. Teachers ask relatively more simple, factual questions of children in low groups and relatively fewer questions that require reasoning. (pp. 89-90)*

Oakes (1986) found the following differences in the treatment of students assigned to either a high or a low ability group:

1. The high ability group was exposed to materials providing substance and challenge—"high-status knowledge" whereas the low ability group read materials containing "low-status knowledge"—less interesting and challenging content.

2. The high ability group was given more opportunity to think critically and solve interesting problems while the low ability group was restricted to memorization and responding to low-level comprehension questions.

3. The high ability group received more instructional time, more homework, and more varied learning activities than did the low ability group.

4. The high ability group received clearer instructions.

5. Low ability students were provided less varied opportunities to learn.

6. High ability students were seen as being more enthusiastic about reading.

7. Low ability students were likely to develop a negative perception of school.

Others have found the following:

1. Cazden (1979) found that teachers had lower expectations for students in the low ability group.

2. McDermott (1976) discovered that teachers were more tolerant of interruptions during instruction with the low ability group.

3. Stoodt and Costello (1986) noted the phenomenon that children in low groups tended to have lower "social maturity"—they attended to instruction less, were frequently non-responsive to questions, and tended to be more impulsive.

4. Hiebert (1983) found that low ability students typically make less progress than students in higher groups. They needed more direct instruction to learn effectively and less time working alone or in small unsupervised groups.

The Self-Fulfilling Prophecy

Jongsma (1985) and Oakes (1986) research revealed that the assignment of a reader to a low ability group was often accompanied by a loss of social status, lowered self-esteem and aspirations, and fostered negative attitudes toward school. Oakes further found that students placed in the low ability group in elementary school were likely to continue in these same groups throughout junior and senior high school. These students were typically placed in non-college preparatory tracks.

Anderson, et al (1985) have written:

> *Whatever cute name may be given to a reading group, the children know their place. They evaluate their own abilities on the basis of the status of their group. The low-group students in one school may be at the same reading level as the students in the average group in another school. Yet, the low-group students in the one school may view themselves as poor readers, and their teachers may have lower expectations for their progress. (p. 89)*

Grouping Practices in Reading Instruction

Whole Group Instruction

Basal reader: The teacher has her entire class go through the same instructional procedures and story readings together. Individuals with special needs receive additional instructional assistance. Supplementary activities may vary to accommodate individual needs.

Problems?

Basal reader team teaching: The teachers at any given grade level group their children by shared abilities and trade for instruction. For example: Teacher A teaches all of the children with "low reading abilities"; Teacher B teaches all of the children with "average reading abilities"; and Teacher C teaches all of the children with "high reading abilities."

Problems?

Literature-based: The teachers do the same as above only use multiple copies of children's books.

Other:

    A. Read-aloud stories

    B. Choral reading

    C. Strategy instruction

    D. Group story writing

    E. Poems

    F. Newspaper reading/magazine reading

    G. Sharing literature extensions

    H. Content-based material

Skill/Strategy Groups

This type grouping is based upon diagnostic and observational information related to a pupils' strengths and weaknesses. Such grouping brings together a small number of readers for a specific purpose. Once the skill or strategy is "mastered," the group is disbanded.

Interest Groups

Groups may be formed on the basis of common interests. If group members are on different instructional levels, cooperation between members can increase motivation and self-satisfaction. Many activities lend themselves to interest grouping:

A. Students who read books by the same author can research that author's life or style of writing, compare stories, or complete artwork related to their books.

B. Students who are interested in a particular subject can come together and read various books on their instructional level and prepare a written or oral group report.

C. Students can listen to a recorded story and/or watch a filmstrip about a particular topic together.

Research Groups

This is similar to interest grouping. Under research grouping, students collect, organize, and synthesize information from a variety of sources and produce a final product (oral report, written report, art activity, etc.).

Cooperative Learning Groups

See attached handout.

Literature Groups

Students of similar abilities and potential interest are given a "book talk" about a novel by the teacher. The novel should be within acceptable parameters of readability. Students opt to read or not read the book. Students who choose to read the book receive introductory lessons and follow-up activities based upon the novel. Those who do not choose to join the group might be involved in IRP.

Cooperative Learning

Definition

Structured activities where positive peer interaction and the achievement of mutual goals are promoted through small-group activities which dovetail with stated curricular objectives. It typically contains four steps: 1) defining the learning task; 2) assigning students to groups; 3) having students compete the learning task in their groups; and 4) letting the groups share their results.

Prerequisites

The classroom teacher needs to create activities that encourage and model: 1) getting to know and trust group members; 2) communicating accurately and unambiguously; 3) accepting and supporting one another, and 4) constructively resolving conflicts to make mutual achievement of goals possible (Johnson & Johnson, 1989/1990).

Examples

1. Before they read a particular passage, give students a list of words that may be unfamiliar. Have each cooperative learning group try to define the words and generate a sentence that uses each correctly. Then get back together and compare definitions and sample sentences.

2. After the children have read a chapter in a content area text, give students a list of statements about the topic of the chapter. Have each group determine whether the various statements are supported by the information in the chapter. Also have them record any supporting information.

3. After the children have read a chapter in a content area text, give students a list of statements about the topic of the chapter. Have each group determine whether the various statements are explicitly supported by information in the text, or whether they require inferences to be made.

4. Before they read a story or article on a particular topic, have students in each group list all of the information they already know about this topic. Then get back together and compare notes.

5. After the students have read a story, have them work together in groups to complete a designated follow-up activity (e.g., responding to comprehension questions, designing a mobile of episodes, etc.)

6. After the children have read a story, have students work in groups to develop a short script from one portion of the selection. Let them practice reading their parts several times before sharing the scripts with the rest of the class.

Use with Exceptional Children

1. D. Johnson and R. Johnson (1984 & 1986) found that involving handicapped and non-handicapped peers in situations in which they must cooperate with one another leads to better

attitudes on the part of the non-handicapped toward their handicapped peers as well as better attitudes of handicapped students toward themselves.

2. Slavin (1983) found that, in order for there to be a positive effect on the achievement of handicapped and low-ability students, cooperative learning must involve two elements: 1) There must be group incentives; and 2) there must be individual accountability. What should be avoided are situations in which the group's solution to a problem can be found by just one or two members. One way of doing this is to base rewards on the group's average so that each individual's score contributes to the total score of the group.

3. Johnson and Johnson (1984) compared competitive, individualistic learning situations to working cooperatively with peers. They found that cooperative group learning:

   1. Will create a pattern of promotive interaction, in which there is

      A. more direct face-to-face interaction among students;
      B. an expectation that one's peers will facilitate one's learning;
      C. more peer pressure toward achievement and appropriate classroom behavior;
      D. more reciprocal communication and fewer difficulties in communicating with each other;
      E. more actual helping, tutoring, assisting, and general facilitation of each other's learning;
      F. more open-mindedness to peers and willingness to be influenced by their ideas and information;
      G. more positive feedback to and reinforcement of each other; and
      H. less hostility, both verbal and physical, expressed towards peers.

   2. Will create perceptions and feelings of

      A. higher trust in other students;
      B. more mutual concern and friendliness for other students, more attentiveness to peers, more feelings of obligation to and responsibility for classmates, and desire to win the respect of other students;
      C. stronger beliefs that one is liked, supported, and accepted by other students, and that other students care about how much one learns and want to help one learn;
      D. lower fear of failure and higher psychological safety;
      E. higher valuing of classmates; and
      F. greater feelings of success.

Other Research

1. Wood (1990) lists well-documented evidence suggesting that cooperative learning contributes to:

   A. Higher motivation to learn and greater instrinsic motivation;
   B. Academic improvements;
   C. Increased self-esteem;
   D. More positive perceptions about the intentions of others;
   E. Decrease of negative competition;
   F. Greater acceptance of differences;
   G. Decreased dependence on the teacher; and
   H. Higher achievement test scores.

2. Cooperative learning promotes race relations (Brandt, 1989/1990).

3. Cooperative learning promotes time and task (Meyers, 1989).

Chapter Three

Holistic Approaches to Reading

Whole Language

Definition

Whole language is a child-centered, holistic philosophy of learning and teaching which recognizes that language learning is both contextually and socially determined, and is constructive in nature. It provides children with a wide range of meaningful language and literary experiences across the entire curriculum, includes evaluation and parent involvement and facilitates the development of responsible, cooperative and caring individuals for whom language is a source of increasing empowerment.

From: Norma Mikleson, University of Victoria, Centre for Whole Language, Victoria, Canada. Presentation April 30, 1989 International Reading Association, New Orleans.

It is a set of beliefs with associated practices!

Beliefs

- Language is purposeful.

- Literary experiences should be authentic.

- Literary experiences can be both personal and social.

- Authentic assessment procedures are more valuable than traditional standardized measures. Children, teachers, and community interact to assess process and product.

- No strict, linear set of skills are requisites for literacy acquisition.

- Curriculum and instruction are based upon developmentally-appropriate understandings.

- Once children are able to identify words independently, practice best facilitates literacy proficiency.

- Parents lay the groundwork for literacy proficiency.

- Intrinsic motivation is the best kind of motivation.

- Literacy learning should be enduring.

- All of the language arts are interrelated.

- Learning about the real world is essential for successful literacy programs.

Practices

- Reading to children

- Shared book experiences

- Sustained Silent Reading
- Integrated Curriculum Units
- Individualized Reading
- Language Experience Approach
- Reader's/Writer's Workshop
- Writing Process
- Journal Writing
- Literature groups
- Portfolio assessment
- Balanced decoding: Sight words, phonics, context clues, structural clues

The Language Experience Approach (L.E.A.)

LEA: The Word Bank

Materials Required

5 x 8 index cards

Index card file

Black marking pen

Personal word books

Procedures

1. Each day each child is asked to tell the teacher a new word he or she would like to learn to read.

2. That word, along with other words housed in the child's Word Bank, are practiced by the child. Words can be practiced in several ways:

   A. Oral recitation
   B. Several children combine the contents of their Word Banks and sort through the pile to find their own words (print names on the backs of cards)
   C. The child may practice writing and saying their words while writing them on the chalkboard or in a tray containing fine sand or cornmeal
   D. The child may trace over the letters of the word while saying the parts of the word aloud.
   E. "D" above could be followed by the child trying to spell the word from memory on the chalkboard or another piece of paper
   F. Two children may form a partner group. Each child tries to teach his own word to the other child

3. Every other day the teacher reviews the words with each child. Words that are not remembered are not kept in the Word Banks but are dismissed as not being important enough to keep.

4. The teacher may want to put a check mark on the back of each word that is remembered. After the child has successfully read his word "X" number of times (10-20), the child may take the card home. (Parents should make a "big deal" about it!) The word can then be entered into his Personal Word Book to use in writing.

Extension

1. *Retrieving words from the floor.* The children's words (usually the words of a group or half of the class is best) are placed on the floor face down. On the signal, each child is to find his own word, hold it up, and tell it to whomever is watching.

2. *Claiming the cards.* The teacher selects many words from the class, holds them up, and the child who "owns" each word claims it.

3. *Telling stories spontaneously.* The child attempts to tell a story about his word. The story could be recorded and transcribed.

4. *Classifying words.* Certain kinds of topics (e.g., desserts, television characters, funny words, places, animals, etc.) are chosen. Topics are selected according to classification. All of the children who have an "animal" word, for example, would stand in one spot. The teacher might want to label the spot with a sheet of paper that says, "animals." Children who have words of other classifications also stand in their designated areas.

5. *Relating words.* Children play this game to see how some words are related to others. For example, someone may have the word "cake" and someone else may have the word "knife." In such a case, a child may say that a knife can cut a cake.

6. *Coauthorship.* Two or more children can get together and combine their words to make longer and longer stories about their original words.

7. *Pass-it-on stories.* A group of no more than five children select words from their Word Banks. For example, they might select such Halloween words as "witch," "haunted," "bats," etc. The first child in the group will write the title; the next child the starting of the story; each child in the group adds something new to the story. The teacher and children can chorally read the story upon completion.

8. *Acting out words.* If the word is conducive to "acting out," a child could dramatize his word for the others to guess.

The Individually Dictated Story: A Combination Technique

Steps

1. Present the child with a stimulus event that you believe would be of interest.

2. Discuss with the child potential elements that could be included in a story or description of the event/object.

3. Have the child tell a short story or describe the object of focus while you take dictation. I have found that a computer with the capabilities of font expansion is best.

4. If possible, wait until the child's thought is complete, then record exactly what the student said.

5. Say each word as you type/write it, asking the student to watch.

6. As you record, provide some reading instruction appropriate for this student (e.g., note that there are spaces between words, that certain words being the same way, that the story has an excellent beginning, and so on).

7. When the child has completed his dictation, read the story aloud to him with expression.

8. Combine elements of the *Neurological Impress Method* with the *Method of Repeated Readings:*

   A. Using your finger to track the print as you read, read the story together for the first time. You should read a little faster and slightly louder than the child.
   B. Continuing to use your finger to track the print, do a second reading of the story this time doing unison reading.
   C. Conduct a third reading of the story this time allowing the child to read the story alone. Have the child track the print with his finger. Any words not recognized after several seconds should be pronounced for the child.
   D. Have the child practice reading the story silently.
   E. When the child is confident about story knowledge, have him read his story to several other people (peers, parent volunteers, your principal, etc.). Require them to get signatures on the back of their story.

9. After the child has had several days of story practice, add the story to his language experience folder. Stories accumulated in the folder should be re-read on a regular basis (once per week).

Extensions

1. Create cloze passages using these stories to provide practice in using context clues and writing frequently-used or favorite words.

2. Select words to focus on—sight words that appear in repeated frames, words that have the same initial sound, base words used in interesting ways—whatever is inherently "teachable" in the story!

3. Try to bring in literature that is related to the "theme" of the dictated story. Read these to the child, or tape record them as a listen-read procedure. Encourage the child to attempt the reading of these materials if possible.

A Skunk Named Flower

by Matt T.

Once upon a time there was this skunk named Flower. He was a little stinker! One Saturday morning Flower took a walk in the woods.

In the woods he met his friend Odor Eater. Odor Eater was in a bad mood that morning and called Flower a very bad name. Flower's feelings were hurt so he did what skunks do best: He squirted Odor Eater.

"Now that's Flower Power!" said Flower. And he left Odor Eater to stink up the forest.

The Use of the Language Experience Approach Group Experience Charts

1. Discuss some event or object of interest to the children. Inform the children that they will be writing a story about it.

2. The children cooperate in dictating the story to the teacher. The teacher writes down the story using the following methods:

    A. Use manuscript handwriting.
    B. Use a heavy writing instrument such as a felt tip pen.
    C. Use chart or butcher paper for recording.
    D. Use the language of the students—do not attempt to alter it.
    E. Make sure students see the words as they are being written.
    F. Try to adhere to the one important event/object and follow a sequence of events.
    G. In beginning each new sentence, emphasize the fact that you start on the left and proceed to the right.
    H. Emphasize the return sweep from the end of one line to the beginning of the next.

3. After the story has been completed, reread it as a choral exercise. Either you or a child may point to each word as it is read. It is important that the word being read is the same one being pointed to.

4. Have individual children take turns rereading the story sentence by sentence.

5. Experience stories are displayed in the room and reviewed on a daily basis for as long as deemed appropriate by the teacher.

LEA Activities

Whole Group

1. Make name labels with the first and last names of the students. Make a chart of the names as they appear on the labels. Have students match the labels with the names on the chart.

2. Make helper charts, using the names as they appear on the name labels. Have each student find his job, matching his/her name label with the chart. At first, pictures may be used to name the jobs. Later, pictures with words may be used, Finally, just words may be used.

3. Read stories to the children and leave the books where the children can look at them independently.

4. Use children's drawings and write sentences dictated by the children on them. Display the pictures or make books of them.

5. Bring something into the classroom that will generate language from the children. Develop a Group Experience Chart.

6. Take a walk to see fall colors, snow, or other seasonal conditions. On return, students list all the words they can that describe the subject of investigation. Students can write about their experience using their writing for reading and sharing.

7. Have a guest speaker speak to your class. The class prepares a list of questions for the speaker in advance. After the visit a thank you letter is composed.

Small Group

1. Have the children dictate a group story. Give each child a copy and have each read the story and underline the words he or she knows. At a later session, the process is repeated. The child again underlines the known words so that there are double lines under the ones remembered.

2. Use children's word banks to play word games such as: Match words that have the same beginning letters or beginning sounds; categorize words (e.g., animals, actions, feelings, etc.).

3. Show a film or filmstrip without narration. Have the children dictate the action while you copy this down.

4. Have the group members make puppets and write a script for a puppet play. The children will rehearse and eventually put on the play.

Individual Activities

1. Have the child dictate his own story while the teacher either carefully writes or types (using a primary typewriter) the child's story. The child practices the story and reads it to others.

2. Have each child make his/her own book of the stories he has dictated. When he/she gets to dictating stories several pages long, each story can be a book by itself.

3. After reading several alphabet books make up his/her own alphabet book.

4. Have each student grow a plant under special conditions such as no light, upside down, sideways, etc. A diary is kept of the project.

5. Have each student pretend he/she is from another planet. He/she may write a news account of his arrival on Earth.

Advantages of the Language Experience Approach

1. The first reading experiences are successful because they use the everyday language patterns of the children. Children who speak a nonstandard language are not penalized or made to feel inferior because they do not measure up verbally to the standard. Likewise, children whose language patterns are beyond those expected are not frustrated by the task of having to learn simpler sight words.

2. The approach is very economical.

3. Children can utilize the sight vocabulary they bring to school.

4. It is individualized in that each child is working at a level he/she can comprehend and with words he/she understands and can recognize.

5. Children learn that listening, writing, and spelling are a part of the reading process and, thus, that the language arts are interrelated.

6. Both phonics and sight words are used. Children see the relationship of sounds to the symbols used to represent them in writing.

7. Children learn to make choices and to function independently as they work with the skills.

8. Children feel their ideas are respected and accepted. This helps develop a positive self-image.

9. Motivation for and interest in reading are greatly increased, which may result in a positive attitude toward reading and creative expression.

10. Children are motivated to increase their spoken and written vocabulary.

11. When the approach is used with the basal program, the teacher may find that many of the words found in the prrprimer may actually be learned before the books are presented.

12. Children may have insight into what goes into a story and can critique and discuss the writer's ideas because they, too, are writers.

13. Children's writings enable the teacher to learn more about the children themselves.

Individualized Reading Program (I.R.P.)

Steps in the Individualized Reading Program (I.R.P.)

1. **Selecting:** the child chooses materials based upon two criteria:

    a. He or she likes the book.
    b. He or she can read it. (See *Rule of Thumb*)

2. **Planning:** the child decides whether or not to read the book.

3. **Independent Work:** the child

    a. Reads a number of books (picture books) or chapters (chapter books).
    b. Plans an extension/sharing activity on one of the latest books/latest chapter read.

4. **Individual Conference:** the child meets with the teacher to:

    a. *See the following page*

5. **Minilessons:** based upon observations made in conferences, the teacher forms groups for instructional purposes based upon demonstrated instructional needs (e.g., context clues, inference, etc.)

6. **Extension:** the child

    a. Completes the activity delineated in 3.b.

Rule of Thumb

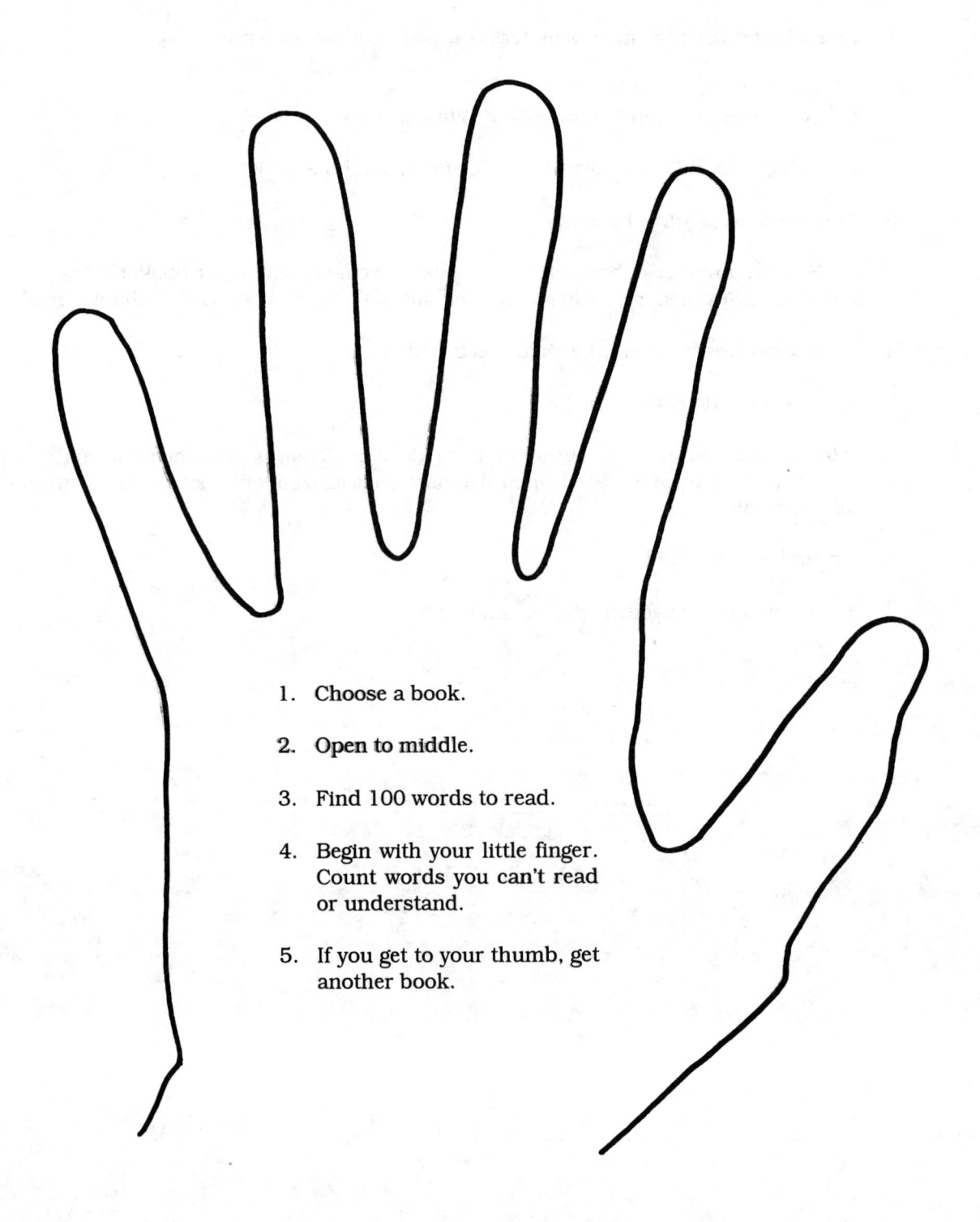

1. Choose a book.

2. Open to middle.

3. Find 100 words to read.

4. Begin with your little finger. Count words you can't read or understand.

5. If you get to your thumb, get another book.

Steps in a Reading Conference

1. **Rapport:** Make sure the child is at ease by some friendly, welcoming comment or question.

2. **Sharing:** Listen as the child tells something about his response to the book he wishes to talk about. Discuss any related activity he may be pursuing.

3. **Question:** Ask one or two searching, general questions concerning the theme of the book, the author's message or point of view, or the nature of the characters.

4. **Oral reading:** Listen to the child read a short passage he has selected to share with you.

5. **Records:** Check the child's *Reading Log* and make appropriate entries into your *Reading Conference Record* concerning progress, interests, and problems. Make note of specific skill necessities in order to form instructional group(s) in the future.

6. **Encourage and guide:** Discuss plans for the future. Offer suggestions about selections of books.

Student Name: _____ Grade: _____ Year: _____

Date	Title	Author	Response	I read this book to myself	I shared this book out loud

Reading Conference Record

Name of Student _____   Date _____

Name of Book _____   Approximate Level _____

How well child enjoyed this book: Very well ___ Some ___ Not very well ___

Appropriateness of child's selection: Good ___ Too easy ___ Too hard ___

COMPREHENSION: General understanding of book: Good ___ Fair ___ Poor ___

	Very good	**Good**	**Fair**	**Poor**
Literal Level Questions	___	___	___	___
Inferential Level Questions	___	___	___	___
Critical Level Questions	___	___	___	___
Creative Level Questions	___	___	___	___

ORAL READING: Fluency: Good ___ Fair ___ Poor ___

___ Word-by-word reading
___ Poor phrasing
___ Lacks good sight vocabulary
___ Reversals
___ Frequent hesitations
___ Nonsense Words inserted
___ Ignores errors
___ Uses monotone when reading

___ Ignores punctuation
___ Repetitions
___ Omissions
___ Insertions
___ Makes errors on easy words
___ Confuses similar looking words
___ Loses place frequently

WORD RECOGNITION: General accuracy of word perception:

Good ___ Fair ___ Poor ___

Needs help in:

___ Development of adequate sight vocabulary.
___ Rapid recognition of common words.
___ Use of contextual information.
___ Use of specific graphophonic patterns.
___ Use of structural analysis.
___ Specific locational errors (initial, medial, final).

SUMMARY AND RECOMMENDATIONS:

Sample Comprehension Questions for Fiction

Please Note: Depending on the level of readers, you may wish to conference prior to, during, or after reading the story. Select a few questions from the one listed below. You may ask any of these questions during shared reading as well.

A. Sequence of Events

1. Tell me what happened first, what happened next, and what happened last. (Continue prompting student; accept the "gist" of the story.)

2. What happened (after/before) _____?

B. Summarize Major Events of the Story

1. Tell me in a few sentences what the story is about.

2. What happened in the story?

3. Why did _____ happen?

4. What was the problem the story was trying to solve?

5. What are some of the important episodes in the story?

C. Predict What Will Happen Next

1. Before reading, predict what the story will be about from the title and/or illustrations.

2. What do you think will happen next?

3. Why do you think that?

4. Find details in the story that support your guess or prediction.

D. Backs up Statement with Proof from Reading

1. Which part of the story best describes _____?

2. See No. 3 above.

3. What made you think _____?

4. How did you know _____?

5. Did you notice any patterns in the story?

E. Connects and Builds to Draw Conclusions

1. What was the problem the story was trying to solve?
2. What do you think the story was trying to tell you?
3. How did the story make you feel?
4. Do you know any other stories that are trying to tell you the same thing?
5. If you could change any part of the story around, what would it be?
6. How did you know_____?

F. Uses Prior Knowledge to Form an Opinion

1. Was this a good story? Why/why not?
2. What was your favorite part(s)? Why?
3. Who was your favorite character(s)? Why?
4. Did you ever have an experience like the characters in the story?
5. Would you like to be any of the characters in the story? Why/why not?
6. Would any of your friends like this book? Why/why not?

G. Evaluates/Judges Characters, Authors, and Books

1. What does the author do to make you read on to find out what happens?
2. Did the story end the way you expected it to? What clues did the author give?
3. Is there anything that makes this author's story unique and different?
4. How does the author make the characters seem real?
5. Is the (main character) like anyone you ever knew? In what ways?
6. Is the (main character) unlike anyone you ever knew? In what ways?
7. Is he or she like you? How?
8. What caused the character to behave in the way he or she did?
9. Is there any way in which the characters changed during the story? How?
10. Describe the other people or character or animals in the story?
11. How did they get along with one another?

12. What problems or troubles did the characters have to overcome?

13. How did they solve their problems?

H. Understands Cause and Effect

1. Why did _____ happen in the story?

2. What caused (the event)?

3. What was the problem in the story? How did the characters find a solution?

4. What caused the character to behave the way he/she did?

I. Connects Experiences with Books

1. Did you ever have an experience like the one in the story?

2. Would you like to be like one of the characters? Why?

J. Identifies Selection/Genre

1. Could this story really happen? Is the story real?

2. Was there any part of the story that you think could not happen in real life? Why?

3. How did the author make the story seem real?

K. Identifies the Elements of Story Grammar

1. How can you tell where and when the story took place? (setting)

2. If you were to paint a picture of the setting, what would you included in your picture? (setting)

3. What gave you clues as to when the story took place? (setting)

4. Which part of the story best describes (setting, character, plot, theme)?

5. Is there a character you know more about then any other? Describe the character. (character)

6. Does the title suit the story or book? Why? (theme)

7. If you could give the story a new title, what would you call It? Why? (theme)

8. Who told the story? How do you know? (point of view/voice)

Fiction Comprehension Checklist
Identifying Elements of Story Grammar

Name _____ Date _____

Selection _____ Oral or Silent _____

	Unassisted Retelling	Assisted Retelling
— PLOT —		
SUMMARIZES AND SUPPORTING EVIDENCE The child identifies main idea/details. (What is the story/passage about? What is the main idea? Give supporting details.)		
SEQUENCING The child identifies the sequence of events. (What happened first? What happened next? What happened last?)		
CAUSE AND EFFECT The child recognizes cause and effect relationships. (Why did _____ happen?)		
DRAWS CONCLUSIONS, USES PRIOR KNOWLEDGE The child makes inferences. (Why do you think _____?)		
GENRE The child can identify the selection as fiction or nonfiction. (Could this story have really happened? Why or why not?)		
PREDICTIONS The child can predict outcomes. (What do you think will happen next?)		
USES PRIOR KNOWLEDGE The child can relate a similar experience that happend to them.		
— CHARACTERS —		
STORY GRAMMAR The child can identify the main and supporting characters. (Who was the main character? Who else was important in the story?)		
STORY GRAMMAR The child can describe the characters. (What was _____ like?)		
EVALUATES The child understands the relationship of the characters to one another and events. (How did _____ feel about? How did _____ feel when _____ happened?)		
— SETTING —		
STORY GRAMMAR The child can identify the story setting. (Where and when did story take place?)		

— SUMMARY —

Level of comprehension: Full and detailed ☐
  Partial ☐
  Fragmentary ☐

Comments: _____

_____

An Introduction to Reader's Workshop: A New Way to Individualized Reading

Reader's Workshop: A Sample Day

The Mini Lesson

"Fact or Fiction"

1. Read the book "Sleeping Ugly" to the students.

2. Engage in a discussion as to whether or not this story "could really have happened."

3. Discuss the categories of "Fact or Fiction" with the students.

4. Have the students volunteer other books that would be considered to be "fiction."

Reading and Responding

1. Students read their books.

2. After reading, the students respond to the attached *Response Chart*.

Share Circles

1. Volunteers share their *Response Charts* with their peers.

Literature Response Chart
Fact or Fiction

Some stories that are written could have actually happened, while others could not. Stories that could have happened are "Fact," while stories that could not have happened are called "Fiction." Read your book. When you have finished or it is 9:40 A.M., use the butcher paper in the Art Center to cartoon one thing that happened in your story that shows it was either "Fact" or "Fiction." Write a caption for your cartoon drawing.

Sleeping for 100 years is not likely to happen.

Illustration by Diane Stanley reprinted by permission of Coward-McCann, Inc. from SLEEPING UGLY by Jane Yolen, illustrations © 1981 by Diane Stanley.

Literature Response Chart
Comparing and Contrasting

Comparing stories, comparing characters, and thinking about how a story is like real life can show you how authors put their stories together.

1. What does the story you just read have in common with other stories? Explain. (Think about the setting, characters, plot, ending, and so on.)

2. Choose two characters from the story. Draw the characters and write how they are alike. How are they different?

Literature Response Chart
Author's Purpose

Sometimes authors write a story to teach you something. Sometimes they just want to entertain you. Sometimes they want to express an opinion. Or they may have another reason.

1. Write why you think the author wrote the story you read. Explain how you know this.

Literature Response Chart
Drawing Conclusions

Sometimes you have to read between the lines in a story to get the whole picture.

1. Select a character from the story. Is she/he a nice person? Explain.

2. Would you like to have this character as a friend? Why or why not?

3. What was the problem this story was trying to solve? Explain.

Literature Response Chart
Summarizing

Knowing the main idea of a story shows you understand the characters and plot.

1. Write who the story is about and what happened to them.

2. Write a newspaper article about the story.

Literature Response Chart
Prior Knowledge

Prior knowledge is using what you already know help you understand the story.

1. Draw a picture and/or write about an experience you had like a character from the story.

2. Would you like to be any of the characters in the story? Explain why.

3. Does the story remind you of any other story? Explain your answer.

Share Circles

Share Circles can be with the whole class, small group, or between partners. These sessions are designed to allow students to:

- Celebrate their reading successes.
- Communicate what was learned from reading.
- Explain the transformation of the reading into a project.
- Make and evaluate an oral/visual presentation.
- Practice listening and responding with questions and compliments.
- Share their "responding to literature" activity.

The Novel Unit

The Novel Unit:
A Literature Approach to Reading

"One of the best kept secrets in education is that children learn to read by reading. Most teachers overreach the skill of reading to the detriment of reading practice and enjoyment. Many primary teachers spend over half of their day teaching children how to read without ever giving them the opportunity for reading."

What You Need:

1. Children.

2. Multiple copies of a good quality children's book.

Before You Form Your Group:

1. Read the book carefully. As you read, note particular *vocabulary* that might best be taught before the reading of a specific section/chapter. (See following page for *how* to select vocabulary for teaching.) Also note the *knowledge* needed to successfully comprehend the material. Make note of *potential disscussion/question items* inherent in the material.

2. Anticipate which children would make a good "match" with the book: The book is readable and might be enjoyed.

Forming the Group:

1. Call up all members of the potential group. Four to ten students are usually involved in a group. You can "bait" the children in a number of ways. One is to give a *book talk*. A book talk involves telling an interesting/exciting part of the book without revealing the outcome. A second way of "baiting" the children is to read the first chapter of the book to the children.

2. Each individual student must make up his or her mind about whether or not to participate in the group experience. I usually let the children take the book home overnight to facilitate decision making.

Pre-reading Activities

1. Generate an interest in the chapter to be read.

2. Develop background knowledge as necessary.

3. Introduce vocabulary (if using DRA).

4. If using *reading response logs*, make the appropriate assignment.

Reading Engagement

1. Allow the children an allotted amount of time to read the chapter.

2. If using *reading response logs*, have the children make their appropriate entries.

Post-reading Activities

Any of the following activities (and others) may be done:

1. Discussion about happenstance in the book.

2. Responding to comprehension questions.

3. Rereading for a specific purpose.

4. Discussion of responses in the students' *reading response logs*.

5. Retelling of specific parts of the story.

6. Illustrating favorite scenes or characters.

7. Acting out the story.

8. Rehearse for a Reader's Theatre presentation.

9. Writing a different ending for the story.

10. Do other activities as suggested in ensuing pages.

Steps in Identifying Vocabulary for Instruction

1. Read the text to determine general story lines or key ideas.

2. Select words that are likely to cause students difficulty in light of students' backgrounds, decoding skills, and abilities to determine meaning. (Examples: "troublemakers," character/place names needing pronunciation assistance.)

3. Identify key-concept words.

4. Identify which key-concept words are adequately defined or contextually identified in the text. These do not have to be pretaught.

5. Identify words for which students can determine pronunciation and meaning by using structural clues. These do not have to be pretaught.

6. Words remaining on the list should be pretaught.

75 Ways to Share a Book

Using the Story

1. Organize a panel to debate it.
2. Dramatize an incident from it.
3. Tell about it over the school PA system.
4. Condense it to *15, 50,* or *100* words.
5. Write about it to a friend.
6. Make a map of where it takes place.
7. Make a story map of its main events.
8. Create a crossword puzzle using its setting and plot.
9. Create a scroll or hand-rolled movie to illustrate it.
10. Tell why it would (or wouldn't) make a great movie.
11. Tell its funniest (or most exciting) incident.
12. Make a poster about it.
13. Pick five to 10 adjectives that describe it. Tell why you chose them.
14. Describe an incident from it as though you were an on-the-scene TV reporter.
15. Make a model of something in it; a house, a log cabin, a rocket.
16. Draw objects from it and make them into a mobile.
17. Draw a significant scene on construction paper cut to the size of a coat hanger; attach it to the hanger; then suspend from the hanger a report about the scene.
18. Choose an idea or scene from it as the subject of a collage. Use old magazine pictures.
19. Make up a limerick or haiku about it.
20. Put an important item from it into a shoebox. Give clues so your class can guess what the item is.
21. Illustrate it with objects found at home or handmade, or with photographs you've taken of people, places, and events.
22. Create a mural about it, using charcoal, crayons, cut paper, water colors, or another art form.
23. Compare it to the movie or TV version.
24. Make a time-line of its events.
25. Create a new ending for it.
26. Make a seed mosaic to illustrate one of its settings or events.
27. Make up a lost or found ad for something in it.
28. Make a peep-box of an important scene or event.
29. Rewrite one of its incidents for a younger reader.
30. Use sketches or photographs to recreate one of its action sequences.

Using Characters

31. The U.S. President has learned that you've read this book and wants to know one thing a main character discovered about life that you think all Americans should know. What would you tell him? Why?
32. Describe the main character in 64 words.
33. Choose a character you'd like (or not like) to have as a friend. Tell why.
34. Make believe you were one of the minor characters. How would you describe a main character?
35. Role-play one of the characters.
36. Plan an appropriate meal for a main character.
37. Do a cartoon strip based on a character.
38. Write a few pages in a diary as if you were one of the characters.
39. Write a poem about a character.
40. Design costumes for some of the characters.
41. Dress as one of the characters.
42. For stories that took place in another time, tell how one of the characters would act today, or would react to a present-day situation.
43. Tell why one of the characters should have had a different role.

Excerpted from *Creating and Managing the Literate Classroom* by Suzanne Barcher. Reprinted by permission of Teacher Ideas Press, 1-800-237-6124.

44. Tell what your home would be like if it belonged to one of the main characters.
45. Write a biography of one of the characters.
46. Write an interview between a character and the author, or between two characters.
47. Create paper dolls of the main characters.
48. Pick a book you think each of the main characters would enjoy reading. Tell why.
49. Prepare flannel-board characters.
50. Develop a game of charades based on the characters.
51. Make puppets of the characters. Set up dialogue.
52. Pantomime a character and ask the class to guess the book.
53. Guess what would have happened if a character had made an important decision differently.

Using the Book Itself

54. Make a list of facts you learned from it.
55. Persuade an audience to read (or not read) it.
56. Tell why you would (or wouldn't) recommend it to your principal, a parent or another student.
57. Tell what the book would say about itself if it could talk.
58. List its five most interesting or critical sentences.
59. Use its theme or setting to create a postcard or greeting card.
60. Compare it to another book the author has written. Describe common elements, style, theme, and so forth.
61. Write a song about it.
62. Demonstrate something you learned from it.
63. Prepare a list of its most unusual, difficult, or exciting words.
64. Use its title and theme to write your own story.
65. Do a scientific experiment associated with it.
66. Present a review of it to a younger class.
67. Pretend to be the book and tell what you hold within your pages.
68. Make a bulletin board about it, showing the main characters, the setting, and so forth.
69. Compare it with a book of similar theme.
70. Prepare a book jacket for it.
71. Have someone who has read it try to stump you with questions.
72. Become the author and tell why you wrote this book.
73. Plan the questions you'd use in a conference-call interview with the author.
74. The author has written to you and wants to know how this book could have been improved. How would you answer?
75. Write a letter of appreciation to the author, asking questions and sharing thoughts.

Literature Response Logs

"A literature response log is a journal for recording reactions to literature" (Routman, 1991). Literature response logs assist in making a logical connection between reading and writing. A response to literature may be intellectual or emotional.

1. Typical audience: End of first grade & up.

2. Responses are directed toward open-ended questions, freewriting, vocabulary words, or illustrations.

3. Materials: Spiral-bound notebook.

4. Use in lieu of workbooks/worksheets.

One Way to Use Literature Response Logs

1. After children have received pre-reading information (e.g., motivation, vocabulary, "backgrounding"), they are given one or more response questions and directed to read a particular literature selection.

2. Children silently read the literature selection.

3. The children respond to the questions in their Literature Response Logs (dated).

4. The children and the teacher meet to discuss the responses the children have made to the posed question(s).

Potential Response Questions

1. Where and when does the story take place? How do you know? If the story took place somewhere else or in a different time, how would it be changed?

2. What incident, problem, conflict, or situation does the author use to get the story started?

3. What does the author do to create suspense, make you want to read on to find out what happens?

4. Trace the main events of the story. Could you change their order or leave any of them out? Why or why not?

5. Think of a different ending to the story. How would the rest of the story have to be changed to fit the new ending?

6. Did the story end the way you expected it to? What clues did the author offer to prepare you to expect this ending? Did you recognize these clues as important to the story as you were first reading it?

7. Who is the main character of the story? What kind of person is the character? How do you know?

8. Are there any characters who changed in some way during the story? If they changed, how are they different? What changed them? Did it seem believable?

9. Some characters play small but important roles in a story. Name such a character. Why is this character necessary for the story?

10. Who is the teller of the story? How would the story change if someone else in the book or an outside narrator told the story?

11. Does the story as a whole create a certain mood or feeling? What is the mood? How is it created?

12. Did you have strong feelings as you read the story? What makes you think of them as you read the story?

13. What are the main ideas behind the story?

14. Is this story like any other story you have read or watched? How?

15. Think about the characters in the story. Are any of them like characters from other stories? Like anyone you've ever met before?

16. What idea or ideas does this story make you think about? How does the author get you to think about this?

17. Do any particular feelings come across in this story? Does the story actually make you think about what it's like to feel that way? How does the author do this?

18. Is there any character that you know more about than any of the others? Who is this character? What kind of person is he or she? How does the author reveal the character to you? What words would you use to describe the main character's feeling in this book?

19. Are there characters other than the main character who are important to the story? Who are they? Why are they important?

20. Is there anything that seems to make this particular author's work unique and different? If so, what?

21. Did you notice any particular patterns in the form of this book? If you are reading this book in more than one sitting, are there natural points at which to break off your reading? If so, what are these?

22. Were there any clues that the author built into the story that helped you to anticipate the outcome? If so, what were they? Did you think these clues were important when you read them?

23. Does the story language seem natural for the intent of the story and for the various speakers?

24. Every writer creates a make-believe world and peoples it with characters. Even where the world is far different from your own, how does the author make the story seem possible?

25. What questions would you ask if the author were here? Which would be the most important question? How do you think the author might answer?

Sustained Silent Reading

1. Students select book(s) to be read for an established period of time. These can be library books, books from home, or books selected from your classroom library.

2. Each student reads alone without disrupting others. No talking or excessive noise is allowed during SSR.

3. Adults within the classroom should also read silently.

4. A sharing period may be allowed after SSR for sharing of interesting and or fun parts of the books read.

"Thematic" Units

When Thematic Units Are Not Thematic Units

Thematic units are omnipresent in today's elementary classrooms. We theme in our units on bears. We theme in our units on monsters. We even theme when we present a unit of study featuring the children's novels of Beverly Cleary. Or do we? The practice of having children systematically studying a topic, a recurring literary phenomenon, or an author's collective works is worthwhile and laudable. It helps children organize their world by providing experiences that are connected by some central focus. However, I contend that educators are using the term thematic unit too broadly. A majority of thematic units developed and presented by teachers are really not thematic units at all. They are centrally focused, but on something other than a literary theme.

Literary Themes

A theme is the underlying idea of a story. It is what remains after the details of the characters, the plot, and the setting have faded away. It is also a unifying phenomenon. Supporting these contentions, Norton (1991) has written that a theme "is the underlying idea that ties the plot, characters and setting together into a meaningful whole" (p. 98). A theme may address specific issues or human conditions. It is the response to the question "what does this story mean?" It is not a concrete object that can be seen. A theme is an abstraction. Stewig (1988) has written:

> After all the details of which people, what places, and when the story happens are stripped away, what a reader is left with is the theme. The theme is the underlying idea, the foundation upon which particular information rests. Theme deals with major issues, such as the importance of standing up for what one believes. Specific details may set the story in the sixteenth or the twenty-first century; the main character may be a young woman or an old man; the environment may be here or in another world. But when these particulars are set aside, the theme of two apparently diverse books may in fact be the same (p. 19).

It should be clear that neither bears, monsters nor Beverly Cleary are themes. Their systematic study involves something other than a theme. An analysis of the types of centrally focused units used by elementary teachers reveals eight different categories of focus. Although there is bound to be a minor amount of overlap in some of the categories, recognition of these categories should assist elementary educators in discussions of what we are using to foster literacy in children. These categories are presented below.

The topical unit. The topical unit is found with great regularity in kindergarten and primary-level classrooms. The topic unit focuses upon a specific concrete phenomenon in nature. Our unit on bears would fit nicely within this category. So would a unit of study on dinosaurs, rocks or weather. A teacher using a topical unit approach would read aloud Milne's Winnie the Pooh and Ward's *The Biggest Bear*, write stories about bears, and integrate the topic of bears into other curricula. The topical unit is perhaps one of the easiest types of unit for teachers to construct. Materials abound for use. A topical unit shows children how literacy resources can contribute to their knowledge of a specific topic. Through this exploration, children should become aware that they can explore books to answer questions they might

From *Reading Horizons*, Vol. 3, No. 3. Reprinted by permission of Reading Horizons, Western Michigan University.

have about a specific topic. However, it should be noted that an appreciation of character, genre, theme or author in the topical unit is ancillary at most. A topical unit teaches about just that: a topic. Literary understanding and appreciation are of secondary concern.

The form unit. Teachers may develop and guide children's explorations of the different forms or genres found in literature. Children are guided through traditional forms of literature such as the folktale, fable, myth and legend, or they might explore poetry, fantasy, contemporary realistic fiction, historical fictions, or tall tales. After hearing, reading and discussing stories such as Bowman's *Pecos Bill, the Greatest Cowboy of All Time* and Kellogg's detail-packed *Paul Bunyan,* children apply what they have learned to write their own form stories. The form unit can identify and clarify the different kinds of literature that exist. This is important in discussions of literature, but can be limited to the extent that grouping literature for study by form may result in reading a number of texts that share nothing in common *other than* genre.

The structural unit. Children may experience literature containing recurring literary structures. Johnson and Louis (1990) have written:

> *The appeal of a structural approach to literature comes from a delight in rhythm and pattern—particularly when the underlying structures aren't immediately evident. Why do so many folk stories have handsome princes and fearsome forests? Why does the Rule of Three appear in folk tales and resurface again and again in modern stories? Why do so many stories involve quests? Why do so many protagonists experience exploration, oppression, struggle, and victory?* (p. 95)

The teacher organizes the literature program around such motifs as quests, heroes, underdogs, evil forces, or family dynamics. Young readers exploring literature about families can compare the Moffats with the Quimbys, or develop an understanding of different family configurations by reading and discussing the problems facing Cadie in Byars' The Pinballs. The structural unit can offer readers an historical perspective of literary components. Structures of literature recur from the heroic quests of Ulysses to the travels of Bilbo Baggins. An understanding of these recurring literary phenomena allows the reader to recognize and appreciate important elements in literature.

The concept unit. Concept units focus upon developmentally relevant concepts. For example, the teacher presents a unit on the concept of changes. Second graders might read and listen to books such as Peet's *The Wump World* and Cooney's *Miss Rumphius* and discuss the different ways change takes place. Fifth graders discover how Sarah not only changes herself, but affects the lives of all of the characters, In MacLachian's *Sarah, Plain and Tall*. Other types of focus might include time, space, exploring, sensing and creating. The concept unit's focus is upon conceptual elaboration and not necessarily upon literary appreciation. This type of unit is, however, useful for children. As changes occur within themselves, for example, they can read related literature revealing that changes are, in fact, normal. They are not odd; all people go through changes. Well-chosen literature can facilitate this understanding.

The picture book unit. The picture book unit is another heavily-used focus of study used by primary school teachers. A trade book, such as Galdone's *The Gingerbread Boy* is introduced to, and read by, participating students. The teacher provides follow-up activities such as writing an alternative ending to the story, taking advantage of the repetitive refrain in the story by having the children engage in choral reading, or cooking gingerbread cookies. The picture book unit is perhaps the simplest of all of the units presented. It can be, however, a pleasant experience for young children. It can be a very positive first experience with the study of literature. In isolation, however, it does not assist children In seeing the connections that do exist in literature. Preferably, teachers will use a particular picture book along with other picture books that share common topics, concepts or structures.

The novel unit. A teacher may select a particular children's novel as a focus of study. Children are guided through a book such as *Julie of the Wolves* by Jean George. Since the novel unit is a lengthy undertaking, teachers involve children in extension activities throughout the unit. Children discuss the theme of humans, with the help from an unlikely source, overcoming the hazards of nature, or they may explore the myths about wolves. Children can experience the art and music of the Innupiat. Traditional Innupiat customs and traditions rediscovered by Miyax can be investigated and discussed. Survival stories can be written by the children. The novel unit can be a rewarding experience for mature primary and intermediate students. As students read a novel, they can discover more about themselves and about life. They can learn different perspectives when they hear different interpretations as shared by their literature group peers. Additionally, meaningful engagement with a substantive work in itself is a worthy objective.

The author unit. A teacher can foster appreciation of a particular author by developing literature units based upon the works of that author. The teacher may involve children in the guided reading of several books written by Bill Peet while reading aloud to the class other selections written by that author. The teacher informs the children about the life of Bill Peet by providing information and reading excerpts from *Bill Peet: An Autobiography*. A "Bill Peet station" is located in the classroom reading center containing a collection of Bill Peet books, book jackets, and illustrations of favorite Peet characters. Self-selection and reading of Peet's books is encouraged. The cultivation of love of author is an important literacy objective. If we are able to "hook" children on a particular author, we can stand back and allow the delightful transaction between reader and author to take place.

The thematic unit. The true thematic unit will focus on a literary theme—an underlying idea that ties the characters, the setting, and the plot together. Children might explore the theme that "friendship assists individuals in overcoming obstacles" by listening to and reading books such as Marshall's *George and Martha*, Lobel's *Frog and Toad are Friends*, and Steig's *The Amazing Bone*. Extension activities might include independent selection and reading of an additional book having the same theme and involving children in composing stories about how friends have assisted them in overcoming obstacles. The concept of theme involves substantial abstractions (Johnson and Louis, 1990). It is important for teachers to consider the amount of abstraction inherent in a particular theme. The theme of "friendship assists individuals in overcoming obstacles" discussed above can be made relatively concrete to younger children because it's likely that they have experienced such a phenomenon. It is less likely that young children will understand the theme of "cooperation is necessary for a society to survive." Care must be taken, therefore, in matching children with age-appropriate thematic material.

Conclusions

Educators are busy developing and implementing units of literary exploration and calling them thematic units. However, few of these units are truly thematic in nature. Eight different types of units involving literature are described here. Each type of unit has a different focus, age-appropriateness, and inherent worth. This descriptive framework may assist teachers in categorizing and discussing the types of literature units they develop and present. It may also assist them in clarifying the central focus of their literature units.

References

Johnson, T.D. & Louis, D.R. (1990). *Bringing it all together: A program for literacy*. Portsmouth: Heinemann.

Norton, D.E. (1991). *Through the eyes of a child: An introduction to children's literature*. New York: Merrill.

Stewig, J.W. (1988). *Children and literature*. Boston: Houghton Mifflin.

Children's Books Cited

Bowman, J.C. (1972). *Pecos Bill, the greatest cowboy of all time*. Chicago: Whitman.
Byars, B. (1977). *The pinballs*. New York: Harper & Row.
Cooney, B. (1992). *Miss Rumphius*. New York: Viking.
Galdone, P. (1975). *The gingerbread boy*. New York: Seabury.
Geroge, J.C. (1972). *Julie of the wolves*. New York: Dutton.
Kellogg, S. (1984). *Paul Bunyan*. New York: Morrow.
Lobel, A. (1970). *Frog and toad are friends*. New York: Harper & Row.
MacLachlan, P. (1985). *Sarah, plain and tall*. New York: Harper & Row.
Marshall, J. (1972). *George and Martha*. Boston: Houghton Mifflin.
Milne, A.A. (1954). *Winnie the Pooh*. New York: Dutton.
Peet, B. (1970). *The Wump world*. Boston: Houghton Mifflin.
Steig, W. (1976). *The amazing bone*. New York: Farrar, Strauss & Giroux.

Dinosaurs

Math
- Make own dinosaur word problems
- Measure dinosaur lengths using string
- Make a frequency chart of students' favorite dinosaur
- Determine the length of each era period
- Measure height using register tape
- Graph differences in weight of various dinosaurs

Music/Drama
- Write own dinosaur rap
- Put on dinosaur puppet show
- Listen to dinosaur songs
- Study sounds dinosaurs made
- Develop a play focusing on a typical day
- Play instruments to copy dinosaur sounds
- Re-enact favorite part of movie
- Write dialogue to picture book to act out

Art
- Make own dinosaur out of paper mache
- Make diorama of area where their dinosaur lived
- Make greeting cards using dinosaur facts
- Create a fossil
- Draw fictitious dinosaurs
- Create an ad to sell a dinosaur
- Build a model of a dinosaur
- Draw time travel vehicle
- Make poster advertising for/against resurrection

Social Studies
- Create a time line
- Study why dinosaurs became extinct
- Chart where different types lived
- Discuss careers of people involved in fossil recovery
- Have an archaeologist speak to the class
- Discuss history of dinosaurs
- Visit prehistoric museum

Physical Education
- "Dinosaur Game"
- Pantomime
- Dinosaur tag
- Dinosaur vs. Human races
- Create aerobic "dinosaur story"

Science
- Create dinosaur exhibit
- Visit a dinosaur exhibit
- Personal speaker
- Study what the dinosaurs ate
- KWLS chart
- Venn diagram comparing meat and plant eaters
- Research skills for comparing attributes
- Video on dinosaur facts
- Guest speaker: DNA specialist

Language Arts
- Story Starters using various books
- Write own story
- Vocabulary crossword
- "If I could be a dinosaur I would be..."
- Create fictitious dinosaur using root words
- Write dinosaur poem
- Journal write from dinosaur perspective
- Journal from archaeologist perspective
- Make dinosaur word chart
- Debate on resurrection issue
- Outlining
- Research
- Note taking

How Do They Explain...

1. The clear success (yes, "empirically") of *Success for All*—a program focusing upon metacognitive skills? (Slavin, et al. 1992, 1994, 1996; Madden, et al. 1993)

2. The clear success (ditto) of *Reading Recovery*—a holistic intervention program for first graders? (Pinnel, et al. 1994)

3. The clear success (ditto) of *Early Childhood Interventions*—a cognitively-based intervention program for young children? (Campbell and Ramey 1994)

4. Marie Carbo's *Reading Styles* program—a program focusing upon children's strengths rather than "deficits"? (Carbo 1996; Snyder 1994; Queiruga 1992)

5. The success of *scaffolding*—a cognitive approach to reading intervention which has been described as "one of the most effective instructional techniques available"? (Graves, Graves, and Braaten 1996)

6. The findings of the National Study of Literature-Based Reading—where it was found that "Literature-based reading causes very significant improvements in reading scores"? (The Institute for Academic Excellence 1993)

7. The impressive success of *transactional strategies instruction*—a cognitive-social set of strategies consistent with Vygotsky? (Brown, El-Dinary, Pressley, and Coy-Ogan 1995)

Chapter Four

Content Area Reading

Metacognition

Definition: Metacognition refers to the knowledge and control which students have over their own thinking and learning activities.

Metacognition in reading refers to three things:

1. **Self-knowledge.** When readers are aware of self in relation to texts and tasks, they are in a better position to use reading strategies effectively.

    A. Do children know what reading is for?
    B. Do they know what the reader's role is?
    C. Do they know their options?
    D. Are they aware of their strengths as readers and learners?
    F. Do they recognize that some texts are harder than others because of their personal knowledge?

2. **Task-knowledge.** Experienced readers are strategic readers. They use their task knowledge to meet the demands inherent in difficult texts. For example, they know how to analyze a reading task, reflect on what they know or don't know about the text to be read, establish purposes and plans for reading, and evaluate their progress in light of purposes for reading. How they read a newspaper will be quite different from how they read a novel.

3. **Self-monitoring.** As we read we monitor our reading progress contingent upon whether or not what we are reading makes sense. This device might be called a *metacognitive sensor*. Fluent reading might be interrupted by this sensor when what we read doesn't make sense.

Where comprehension can break down:

1. Failure to understand a word

    A. Novel word
    B. Known word that doesn't make sense in the context

2. Failure to understand a sentence

    A. Can find no interpretation
    B. Can find only a vague, abstract interpretation
    C. Can find several possible interpretations
    D. Interpretation conflicts with prior knowledge

3. Failure to understand how one sentence relates to another

    A. Interpretation of one sentence conflicts with another
    B. Can find no connection between the sentences
    C. Can find several possible connections between the sentences

4. Failure to understand how the whole text fits together

    A. Can find no point to the whole or part of the text
    B. Cannot understand why certain episodes or sections occurred
    C. Cannot understand the motivations of certain characters

Possible remedies for comprehension breakdowns:

1. Ignore and read on, because this information is relatively unimportant.

2. Suspend judgment because it is likely to be cleared up later.

3. Form a tentative hypothesis to be tested as reading continues.

4. Reread the current sentence(s) or look for a tentative hypothesis.

5. Reread the previous context to resolve the contradiction.

6. Go to an expert source, because it simply doesn't make sense.

General metacognitive teaching suggestions:

1. For content area assignments, let students know the extent to which they should monitor their comprehension. Must it all make sense right away? Should they just try to get the flavor and wait for class to get their questions answered?

2. Always focus on meaning when teaching reading. Use activities that make sense to the students. Use materials that they can understand.

3. Encourage an active approach toward learning by encouraging students to ask questions whenever they do not understand something in class or in their assignments.

4. Try to overcome the students' learned helplessness. Provide situations in which additional effort can make a difference.

5. Teach students that taking risks and making guesses is good. This is an effective strategy in many cases of comprehension breakdown.

6. Teach the students that comprehension can break down at one of four levels: word, sentence, paragraph, or passage. Tell them that the first step is to identify the level in which it occurs.

7. Use explaining and modeling to teach the taxonomy of remedies for comprehension failures. Help students use it when they let you know they are having problems with comprehension.

8. Whenever students come to class with reports of comprehension problems ("I didn't understand it!"), you have an opportunity to teach comprehension monitoring. Don't explain the material to them. Instead, help them remedy the situation by applying strategies.

K-W-L

Sequence

1. The students first recall what they already *know* about an identified topic.

2. The students then think about *what* they want to learn about that topic.

3. Finally, they identify what they have *learned* about the topic after reading.

Rationale

The above sequence is what adept readers do rather casually. This technique helps less adept readers use strategies used by more sophisticated readers.

K-W-L

What I Know	What I want to Know	What Have I Learned?

Adapted from Carr, E. & Ogle, D. (1987). KWL Plus: A Strategy for Comprehension and Summarization. *Journal of Reading, 30,* 626–631.

K-W-L-S

K-W-L (Carr & Ogle, 1987; Heller, 1986; Ogle, 1986, 1992) is a popular activity assisting students in activating background knowledge, structuring inquiry, and summarizing learned information. The *K* represents what students already know about a particular topic, and the *W* represents what students want to know about the topic. Notes about both of these are recorded on a three-column chart before students read. After reading, students enter in the third (L) column what they learned about the topic.

Ogle (1986) originally included two categories of information to be recorded in the third column: What I learned and what I still need to learn. In my work with children, I noticed that they frequently emphasized the "what I learned" component of the third column and minimized the content of "what I still need to learn." Although the two are certainly linked, it would seem clearer for children if they were charted as two separate categories. Thus, I developed K-W-L-S, which is essentially identical to K-W-L with an added fourth column: "what I still need to learn." In this way, readers may attend to what remains unanswered and is worth further inquiry after reading.

The results have been positive. Elementary students include much more "what I still need to learn" information on the four-column chart as compared to the traditional K-W-L chart. K-W-L-S focuses readers' attention more directly upon "what I still need to know" information.

Sippola, A. (1995). K-W-L-S, *The Reading Teacher, 48*, 542–543.

K.W.L.S

What I Already Know	What I Want to Know	What I Learned	What I Still Need to Know

SQ3R

Some Specifics

1. Developed by Robinson in 1946.

2. Seeks to make reading more meaningful by:

    A. Giving the reader some purpose for reading.
    B. Getting the reader to search for information of the answers to questions rather than being passively manipulated by print.
    C. Encouraging review.
    D. Causing students to spend more time on task.

Description

SURVEY: This initial preview step in the method encourages the reader to skim the reading assignment in order to answer broad questions about its content. The reader should spend several minutes quickly reading the opening paragraphs or the chapter, major headings and subheadings, and possibly the chapter summary. Attention should also be directed briefly to pictures, charts, and italicized words. At the conclusion of the survey, the reader should be able to answer questions such as: "What is this chapter about, basically?" or "Is this chapter going to require more study than usual?"

QUESTION: In this second stage of SQ3R, the reader begins to progress sequentially through the text. The reader converts scanned information into questions. For instance, the heading "Characteristics of Alligators" would be transformed into "What are the characteristics of alligators?"

READ: As the readers read, they find answers to their questions.

RECITE: After each section of the chapter is read, the reader pauses briefly to: A) determine whether or not the questions posed in step 2 have been answered satisfactorily, and B) rehearse the answer.

REVIEW: At the end of the chapter, the reader spends a few minutes trying to recall main ideas and important supporting details from the entire reading assignment. The review may also entail paging through the chapter using each heading as a focus. Frequent reviews are recommended to promote long-term recall.

ReQuest

ReQuest, or reciprocal questioning, was created as a remedial technique by Manzo (1969). This technique has been shown to help students think as they read in any situation that requires reading. This technique encourages children to ask their own questions about the material being read.

Steps

1. All "players" (teacher and students) silently read a common segment at the beginning of the selection together.

2. The teacher closes his book, and the students are free to ask the teacher questions about the selection read.

3. The teacher responds to those questions providing reasons why he answered that way.

4. Next, the students close their books and the teacher poses model questions for them to answer.

5. The next segment of the selection is read and steps 3 and 4 are repeated.

6. At a suitable point in the text, the teacher asks the students to make predictions about the rest of the text.

7. Students are then assigned the remaining portion of the selection to be read silently.

8. The teacher facilitates follow-up discussion of the material. Success of predictions is discussed.

Anticipation Guides

An anticipation guide is designed to activate children's thoughts and opinions about concepts to be discussed in a content-are chapter or book. It also focuses the child's attention upon those concepts as they actively read the chapter/book for information.

Steps

1. Identify the major concepts to be learned in the text.

2. Determine how the main concepts support or challenge your children's beliefs.

3. Create three to five statements that support or challenge your children's beliefs and experiences about the topic under study.

4. Arrange the statements on an overhead projector, chalkboard, or ditto sheet in whatever order you think is most appropriate. This may correspond to the order in which the concepts are dealt with in the text.

5. Present the guide to the children. The children are instructed to think about each of the statements, formulate a response to it, and be prepared to defend their opinions.

6. Discuss each statement briefly.

7. Direct the children to read the text, keeping in mind their opinions and other opinions they have heard. They are directed to find out what the text has to say about each statement.

8. Discuss the evidence found in the text.

Sample Anticipation Guide

Directions: Below are some statements about cities. Read each sentence. Do you agree with the statements? If you do, place a + on the line before the statement. If you disagree, place a - on the line before the sentence.

+ 1. Most people live in cities.

___ 2. It is better to live in a city.

− 3. Only the United States has big cities.

− 4. Cities are just the same as **towns**, only bigger.

− 5. People live where they do because they want to.

Cloze Assessment

The CLOZE PROCEDURE can be used to assess student knowledge of technical vocabulary in either a pre- or post-reading situation. Select or construct a passage containing germane technical vocabulary and delete those words.

SAMPLE: Science lesson on living matter

Structures in living things range from simple to complex.

There are "levels of organization" among (1)_____

things. In your earlier studies in (2)_____, you

probably learned about electrons, protons, and (3)_____

and how they are organized into (4)_____.

Perhaps you are familiar with the idea of (5)_____ _____

being organized into molecules, and you may know that

(6)_____, in turn, may be (7)_____

into cell parts such as the nucleus, (8)_____

and cell membrane.

. . . .

(Answers: 1. living; 2. science; 3. neutrons; 4. atoms; 5. atoms; 6. these; 7. organized; 8. cytoplasm.)

Pre-reading Activity
Technical and Common Vocabulary
Farming Regions

Directions: If the two words mean the same, then write *SAME* on the line between the words. If they don't mean the same or if they are opposites, then leave the line blank.

You will participate in this activity before we start to study this topic to see how much you already know. You will engage in this activity again at the end of the unit to see how much you have learned.

drought	_____	dry
grasslands	_____	prairie
farms	_____	stations
middle	_____	central
topsoil	_____	surface soil
wasteland	_____	fertile
natural	_____	man-made
cat	_____	dingo
vegetation	_____	plant life
general	_____	specialize
soybeans	_____	hops
bread	_____	grain elevator
taxes	_____	combine
fallow	_____	bare
replica	_____	similar item

Prediction Guide: Washington

Predict before you read the assigned article. Write either *yes* or *no* on the line **Before** reading. As you read the article, write *yes* or *no* on the line **During** reading.

Before	During		
_____	_____	1.	We will be reading about Oregon.
_____	_____	2.	Mike Lowry is the governor of Spokane.
_____	_____	3.	Cougar fans are, generally, crazy.
_____	_____	4.	Huskies rule.
_____	_____	5.	Olympia is the state capitol.
_____	_____	6.	Cheney is the center of the universe.
_____	_____	7.	*Benny and Joon* was filmed in Nude City, Washington.
_____	_____	8.	Eastern Washington is anyplace east of Seattle.
_____	_____	9.	Forks, Washington is a good place to eat.
_____	_____	10.	Humptullips is a bad concept.

Chapter Five

Special Needs Children

Characteristics of a Learning Disabled Reader

1. Reversals of letters or words. In the case of letters, the student may reverse **b's** and **d's, p's** and **q's,** or less commonly **n's** and **u's,** thus making **bad** read **dab** or **baby** read **dady;** in the case of words, parts of words may be reversed as in **ant** to **nat,** or entire words may be reversed as in **saw** to **was** or **on** to **no.**

2. Short or erratic memory for words. Words that a normal reader would learn in teaching-learning situations may require many more exposures for the disabled reader. Also, a word could be remembered and spoken correctly one time and not recognized the next time. This failure to recognize may occur within a period of minutes.

3. Oral rereading not improved following silent reading or a first oral reading.

4. Inability to hold information in memory until needed. Memory problems are exhibited in the use of context clues; that is, the student cannot remember what has just been read and so cannot derive a new word from context. Problems are also exhibited in use of phonics or structural analysis for word attack. In sounding a word with three phonemes, the student may forget the first one or two by the time the third appears.

5. Difficulty with concentration. Some students simply cannot attend to a paragraph or story as it is being read or cannot listen for periods beyond a half minute. This problem becomes apparent when dealing with abstract relationships such as sound-symbol correspondence. Students with subtle difficulty in concentrating may not have obvious hyperactivity or other behavior problems.

6. Inability to see whole relationships. This difficulty is illustrated by the phonetic speller who is unable to form a mental image of a word. Also, words are often spelled exactly as they sound, e.g., **liks** for **likes** or **hav** for **have.**

7. Emotional instability. Most students become irritated when they fail to experience some success. Students with severe reading disability, however, have a tendency to become extremely irritable on meeting a task at which they are not immediately successful. Their moods may also change rapidly.

8. Impulsiveness. This problem is illustrated by the student who guesses at words rather than working them out using word-attack skills. Impulsiveness is best demonstrated when pictures are presented on a page. The student may say **bunny** for **rabbit** when the word **rabbit** is accompanied by an illustration of a rabbit.

9. Poor eye-motor coordination. This problem can be measured using tests. It can also be noted by observing the student write or engage in motor activities such as cutting with scissors or coloring. Tests have the advantage of providing scoring criteria or norms from which to judge the student's performance. However, the eye of an experienced teacher may be just as capable in identifying eye-motor coordination problems.

10. Difficulty with sequencing. This problem arises in poor spelling but may be more common in reading when the student has difficulty remembering the specific order of words in a sentence, events in a paragraph, days in a week, or months in a year.

11. Inability to work rapidly. This problem arises in reading assignments but is equally common in written work. The student is consistently behind the pace set by others and gets irritable if rushed. There is also a tendency to perseverate, or dwell on a particular point for an extra long time.

12. Omissions of words and phrases. It should be emphasized that many students omit an occasional word, but some severely disabled readers consistently omit words, especially unknown words. There is also a tendency to skip whole phrases or lines and to constantly lose place.

13. Directional confusion. This may show up, as mentioned before, in lack of ability to distinguish b and d, and so forth. Confusion can extend, however, to inability to distinguish left and right, front and back, before and after.

14. Poor auditory discrimination. This condition may be present even when the student's auditory acuity is excellent. Again, many students have difficulty with auditory discrimination, but the severely disabled reader has trouble learning minute differences in words such as **pen** and **pin** or even **him** and **hen.** Disabled readers are also erratic in their ability to discriminate sounds.

15. Hyperactivity. The hyperactive student frequently has a short attention span and is wiggling and squirming, tapping fingers, etc. These signs are more apparent when the student is under stress such as when completing an assignment.

16. Poor syntax, stuttering or halting speech. The student who exhibits speech problems seems to need to think ahead when talking; that is, words do not flow smoothly, or when they do, the order of the words is illogical.

17. Achievement in mathematics is considerably higher than in reading and spelling. Perhaps there is a physiological explanation for this. Some people who have suffered strokes have been left unable to read/spell but still are able to solve difficult math problems.

Attentional Deficit Disorder

The A.D.D. Child: is highly distractible and impulsive. Since the etiology of the problem is the child's unstructured and disorganized approach to most tasks, the first step is to provide a structured, well-organized, nondistracting environment. A regular schedule with minimum interruption is important, as is a consistent approach to learning tasks.

Strategies

1. Seat the child near the teacher's desk in a reassuring, nonthreatening way.

2. Address the child by name before eliciting a response or calling attention to the child. It is helpful to stand near or touch the child when giving instructions to the class or eliciting a response.

3. Remember that physical features of the work environment influence the child's activity and distractibility levels. Consider these guidelines:

   A. Reduce the stimuli in the child's visual field.
   B. Use lighting of medium intensity—no flickering or bright lights.
   C. Plan the schedule so that the child is not expected to concentrate when there is distracting noise in the hallway. Music set at a low volume can be helpful in masking continuous distractions.
   D. Create a private work place by screening off a work area for children with significant attentional deficits.

4. Give shorter assignments with immediate feedback on results. Stress quality, not quantity. An A.D.D. child often has difficulty finishing work.

5. Use techniques that assist the short-term memory. Use an assignment card that is reviewed daily and kept at the student's work area.

   A. List each activity separately. If necessary, list specific steps.
   B. Require that the child have activities checked off as progress is made.
   C. Set approximate time limits for an activity. It may be helpful to provide a timer. However, some children become more disorganized under time pressure.

6. Use techniques for dealing with impulsivity and what appears to be an increased activity level. Immobility for long periods of time is detrimental. The child should be given legitimate opportunities for physical movement.

Diagnostic Criteria for Attention-Deficit-Hyperactivity Disorder (ADHD)

Note: Consider a criterion met only if the behavior is considerably more frequent than that of most people of the same mental age.

A. A disturbance of at least six months during which at least eight of the following are present:

1. Often fidgets with hands or feet or squirms in seat (in adolescents, may be limited to subjective feelings of restlessness).
2. Has difficulty remaining seated when required to do so.
3. Is easily distracted by extraneous stimuli.
4. Has difficulty awaiting turn in games or group situations.
5. Often blurts out answers to questions before they have been completed.
6. Has difficulty following through on instructions from others (not due to oppositional behavior or failure of comprehension). e.g., fails to finish chores.
7. Has difficulty sustaining attention in tasks or play activities.
8. Often shifts from one uncompleted activity to another.
9. Has difficulty playing quietly.
10. Often talks excessively.
11. Often interrupts or intrudes on others.
12. Often does not seem to listen to what is being said to him or her.
13. Often loses things necessary for tasks or activities at school or at home.
14. Often engages in physically dangerous activities without considering possible consequences (not for the purposes of thrill-seeking), e.g., runs into street without looking.

B. Onset before the age of seven.

C. Does not meet the criteria for a Pervasive Developmental Disorder.

Criteria for Severity of Attention-Deficit-Hyperactivity Disorder

Mild: Few, if any, symptoms in excess of those required to make the diagnosis and only minimal or no impairment in school and social functioning.

Moderate: Symptoms or functional impairment intermediate between "mild" and "severe."

Severe: Many symptoms in excess of those required to make the diagnosis and significant and pervasive impairment in functioning at home and school with peers.

Reprinted with permission from the Diagnostic and Statistical Manual of Mental Disorders, Fourth Edition. Copyright 1994 American Psychiatric Association.

Learning Disabilities

Some definitions:

> "Children with special (specific) learning disabilities exhibit a disorder in one or more of the basic psychological processes involved in understanding or in using spoken or written language. These may be manifested in disorders of listening, thinking, talking, reading, writing, spelling, or arithmetic. They included conditions which have been referred to as perceptual handicaps, brain injury, minimal brain dysfunction, dyslexia, developmental aphasia, etc. They do not include learning problems which are due primarily to visual, hearing, or motor handicaps, to mental retardation, emotional disturbance, or to environmental disadvantage." (National Advisory Committee on Handicapped Children, 1968)

> "Learning disability in a generic term that refers to a heterogeneous group of disorders manifested by significant difficulties in the acquisition and use of listening, speaking, reading, writing, reasoning or mathematical abilities. These disorders are intrinsic to the individual and presumed to be due to central nervous system dysfunction. Even though a learning disability may occur concomitantly with other handicapping conditions (e.g., sensory impairment, mental retardation, social and emotional disturbance) or environmental influences (e.g., cultural differences, insufficient/inappropriate instruction, psychogenic factors), it is not the direct result of those conditions or influences." (U.S. Joint Committee on Learning Disabilities, 1981)

(This committee suggested that their definition has several advantages over the federal definition because:

1. It is not concerned exclusively with children;

2. It avoids the controversial phrase "basic psychological processes";

3. Spelling is not included since it is more logically subsumed under writing;

4. It avoids the use of confusing terms such as perceptual handicaps, dyslexia, minimal brain dysfunction; and

5. It clearly states that learning disabilities may occur in conjunction with other types of handicaps.)

Neurological Impress Method

The *Neurological Impress Method* (Heckleman, 1966; 1969) is a technique in which the teacher and student read aloud simultaneously from the same material. Heckleman speculated that such reading together would result in "neurological traces" being formed that would be beneficial to learning. This idea, which seemed rather exotic for its time, is regaining some stature due to the work of neurophysiologists who are reporting that physical webbings are observable in the brain in response to "optimal" levels of stimulation (Diamond, 1989).

Steps

1. The teacher sits slightly behind the student.

2. The teacher reads into the student's preferred ear.(This is usually the right.)

3. The teacher slides a finger under each word being read.

4. The teacher first reads in a slightly louder and slightly faster voice than the student, and, with time, lower and slower, and with the student's finger setting the pace.

5. The teacher does not attempt to teach word analysis at this time.

6. The teacher attempts to provide words in advance of the student's need when it is believed that it will slow the student down, even after the shift to student control of pacing and louder oral reading.

Suggestions

1. As you work with the student, you are likely to notice a sharp improvement in reading ability. Begin to increase your rate of reading as the student's reading improves.

2. Read for periods of five to fifteen minutes two to four times per day. This method can be explained to parents, so they may use the same procedure with the student at home.

Neurological Impress Method + Aspects of Repeated Readings

Step One: The teacher selects a one hundred to two hundred word passage for reading. The materials should be at the child's instructional level.

Step Two: The teacher sits slightly behind the student.

Step Three: The teacher reads into the student's ear (usually the right ear is preferable in that it has stronger connections to the left hemisphere, and does not have to cross the corpus callosum—the hemisphere-connecting fibers—as does sound to the left ear). The teacher slides a finger under each word being read. Care should be taken to have one's finger underneath the exact word being read. The teacher reads slightly faster and louder than the child during this first reading.

Step Four: A second reading of the same materials ensues. The student and teacher do unison reading.

Step Five: A third reading of the same material is done. The child does the oral reading with the teacher only providing a word when the child is unable to recognize the word after one to two seconds.

Pitfalls to Avoid When Using N.I.M.

1. The teacher tends to go too fast or too slow.

2. The story is too long, and therefore so is the activity.

3. The story language is too difficult.

4. The pupil attends more to the teachers voice than the print.

5. The complexity of the story is too difficult.

6. The teacher drills the student on word identification.

7. The teacher lacks appropriate intonation.

Modifications of the Neurological Impress Method

Simultaneous Assisted Reading

1. Children read along with the teacher using either a *big book or* multiple copies of a books written at their "instructional level."

2. The technique is most effective when the material being read is repeated several times.

3. As rereading ensues, the teacher "fades" her assistance.

Echo Reading

1. The teacher reads a sentence or two aloud from materials written at the children's' "instructional level."

2. The students immediately repeat what the teacher read while looking at, and if necessary, pointing to the words.

3. Entire short stories or a number of passages may be used with this technique.

4. Excellent *modeling* is provided to the students.

Choral Reading

1. The teacher leads the students in reading together a literary selection (poetry is exceptionally good for this). All readers read in unison with expression modeled by the teacher.

2. The teacher's voice leads the initial rehearsal. As repeated readings ensue, the teacher "fades" his or her voice.

3. Choral reading promotes expression and fluency in oral reading.

Simultaneous Listening-Reading (Also Known as *Auding* [Chomsky, 1978] and *Listen-Read Procedure* [Sippola, 1988])

1. Children listen to teacher-prepared tape recordings of materials which, at the same time, follow along in the book. Finger pointing is encouraged initially.

2. Appropriate rate of presentation is important as well as careful monitoring.

Method of Repeated Readings

Name _____   Date _____

Book _____

WPM

300									
290									
280									
270									
260									
250									
240									
230									
220									
210									
200									
190									
180									
170									
160									
150									
140									
130									
120									
110									
100									
90									
80									
70									
60									
DATE									
PAGE									
	1	2	3	1	2	3	1	2	3

Directions: Read your story/book at least once. Choose one page for a timed reading. Record the date and page number. Find a partner. Read aloud to your partner while s/he times you for one minute. Record the number of words. Reread each page practiced two additional times. Graph the results.

The Method of Repeated Readings

Name _____   Date _____

Story Read _____

Timing # 1   **Timing # 2**   **Timing # 3**

Miscues   *Miscues*   *Miscues*

Time: ____   Time: ____   Time: ____

Evaluation: _____
_____
_____
_____

Reading in Phrases

Reading in phrases means dividing a sentence into thought units. Phrasing is indicated during speaking or oral reading by pauses (The gracious hostess   moved quietly   among her guests). The key is that the words in the phrase are related in some meaningful way so as to form a thought unit.

A **_prerequisite_** for the ability to read in phrases is the child possessing an adequate sight vocabulary! Without this, the child will not, logically, read in phrases.

Assuming the child has an adequate sight vocabulary and still reads word-by-word, the reading specialist can:

1. Explain and demonstrate to the child what a phrase is, why it is important, and how to phrase (modeling).

2. Model good phrasing. Read sentences orally with somewhat exaggerated phrasing; then have the children imitate your renditions. Having the child read in unison with the teacher, and the alternate reading of sentences aloud by the teacher and pupil are also helpful.

3. Use reading material that is well within the word-recognition and comprehension abilities of the child.

4. Provide practice in reading material in which the phrases have been marked off by vertical lines (The boy/ is going/to the store.), by underlining each phrase (The boy is going to the store.), or by spaces (The boy   is going   to the store.).

5. After the pupil has developed some skill in the use of material that has been phrased for him, he can be asked to mark off the phrases on unmarked selections. His ability to group words into phrases can be checked, and assistance provided as needed.

6. It is important for children to use their newly acquired phrasing skills in their everyday reading. Without frequent practice, they may lose whatever gains were made.

Phrase Reading

What a lot   of hairy-faced men   there are around nowadays.

When a man   grows hair   all over his face   it is impossible   to tell   what he really   looks like.

Perhaps that's why   he does it.   He'd rather   you didn't know.

Then there's   the problem   of washing.

When the   very hairy ones   wash their faces,   it must be   as big a job   as when   you and I   wash the hair   on our heads.

So what I   want to know   is this.   How often   do all thse   hairy-faced men   wash their faces?   Is it only   once a week,   like us,   on Sunday nights?   And do they   shampoo it?   Do they use   a hairdryer?   Do they rub   hair tonic in   to stop their faces   from going bald?   Do they go   to a barber   to have   their hairy faces   cut and trimmed   or do they do it themselves   in front of   the bathroom mirror   with nail scissors?

I don't know.   But next time   you see a man   with a hairy face   (which will   probably be   as soon as you   step out onto   the street)   maybe you will look   at him   more closely   and start wondering   about some   of these things.

From *Twits* by Roald Dahl. Copyright 1981 by Roald Dahl. Reprinted by permission of the publisher, Alfred A. Knopf, Inc.

Individual Vocabulary Method

The *Individual Vocabulary Method* is a modification of the Language Experience Approach (Word Banks) found to be particularly helpful with nonreaders of any age and individuals who have developed an aversion to books due to non-success.

1. The teacher begins by soliciting several important words from each child. (In later sessions, only one word is acquired.)

2. The words are written in neat manuscript handwriting on a large index card using a black marking pen.

3. At the beginning of each session, all of the students' cards are scattered on a table or the floor. The children find their own personal cards. (Hint: Write their names of the backs of the cards.)

4. The children then form reading partners and teach/learn each other's words. While this is going on, the teacher is working with individual children reviewing old words and generating/writing new ones.

5. A *Word Bank* is established. Children use their Word Banks to write stories. These stories are shared with the other students and housed in a class library to be read by others.

Fernald Approach
(V.A.K.T. — Visual Auditory Kinesthetic Tactile)

Audience: Extremely disabled readers: Visually handicapped, neurologically impaired, children with visual-perceptual or visual processing problems.

Stage One

1. The teacher writes a student-chosen word with crayon on a large piece of paper (letters approximately two inches high).

2. The child traces the word with an index finger, saying each part of the word. This is repeated until the child can write the word without looking at the model.

3. After a few words are learned, the child dictates a short story to the teacher using many of his/her words. The story is typed for use on the next day. The words are kept in a folder.

4. Students are drilled each session on the words. When they recognize a word twenty consecutive times, the word is put in a permanent collection (e.g., personal dictionary) and reviewed two times a month.

Stage Two

1. Same as Stage One only tracing is omitted.

Stage Three

1. The child is involved in reading in books. When he or she does not recognize a word in print, it is written down.

2. The teacher records the word on an index card. The card is taught as a sight word.

Stage Four

1. The student is able to recognize new words from their resemblance to word/word parts he or she already knows on the basis of context.

The Language Experience Approach with Remedial Readers

Groups of Students

1. Discuss some event or object or interest to the children. Inform them that they will be writing a story about it.

2. The children cooperate in dictating the story to the teacher. The teacher writes down the story keeping the following in mind:

    A. Use **manuscript** handwriting.
    B. Use a heavy writing instrument such as a felt tipped pen.
    C. Use chart or butcher paper for recording.
    D. Use the language of the students—do not attempt to alter it.
    E. Make sure students see the words as they are being written.
    F. Try to adhere to the one important event/object and follow a sequence of events.
    G. In beginning each new sentence, emphasize the fact that you start on the left and proceed to the right.
    H. Emphasize the return sweep from the end of one line to the beginning of the next.

3. After the story has been completed, reread it as a choral reading exercise. Either you or a child may point to each word as it is read by the group. It is important that the word being read is the same one being pointed to.

4. Have individual children take turns rereading the story sentence-by-sentence.

5. Duplicate the story on a large piece of tagboard and have the students cut it into sentence strips. These can then be put in a pocket chart to form the original story. Go back to the original chart when necessary. Also, let students rearrange the sentences to form a different order of events.

6. After students have read the story over many times, you may wish to cut the tagboard sentences up into words and let students form the original sentences and new sentences.

7. As more stories are dictated and read and as students build a larger sight vocabulary, you may wish to duplicate stories onto copy paper and give each student a copy to be cut up into sentences and/or words for building varying story order and new sentences.

8. As students' reading ability grows, you should begin to let each student write and illustrate his or her own stories. These can be bound into booklets with attractive covers on them indicating the author of each book. Students should then begin to reading each other's books.

9. A great deal of emphasis should always be placed on rereading materials that were written earlier, as children require a great many exposures to each word before it becomes a sight word. After sight vocabularies begin to grow considerably, students can begin to read trade books.

Individual Students

1. As with a group, find some event or object of interest to the student and ask him to dictate a story or description to you.

2. As the student dictates, you print or type the story on a piece of paper with the student positioned so that he may observe the writing or typing.

3. Do either unison or echo reading of the story. Point to the words being read.

4. Repeat #3 several times.

5. Let the student illustrate the story or apply stickers, pictures, or other decorations. Finally, the story should be placed in a booklet to be kept and reviewed frequently.

6. You may wish to duplicate the typewritten copies of these stories so that the student can cut them up and rearrange first the sentences and later the words within each sentence.

7. Bind groups of stories into booklets with illustrated covers and encourage children to exchange and read each other's booklets.

8. Gradually encourage the student to branch out into the reading of trade books.

Diagnosis and Remediation: Some Specifics

Deficiencies	Possible Causes	Corrective Measures
Poor word recognition	Material too difficult. Too little phonics and other methods of word attack. Lack of knowledge about English. Visual deficits. Low mental abilities. Scarcity of reading materials. Poor teaching.	Drill on common sight words through spelling, games, stories, flash cards, tachistoscope, sentences, phrases, and much reading of easy materials. Correct physical defects if possible. Teach methods of word attack. VAKT.
Reading word-by-word	Classroom methods that overemphasize oral reading. Material too difficult. Poor vision. Insufficient phrase drill. Unable to get words through context.	Silent reading and discussion before oral reading. Easy, attractive reading materials. Correct visual defects. Use a variety of methods in teaching sight vocabulary.
Inability to attack new words and unfamiliar words	Weakness in auditory perception. Lack of training in word analysis. Ineffective teaching.	Teach pupil how to read words through the use of context, phonics, structural analysis.
Pointing with finger	Visual defects. Materials too difficult. Uses as a crutch to aid in holding place. Poor beginning teaching methods. Nervousness.	Lead pupil to see that it retards his/her speed. Use easy, attractive material. Use a marker (index card) to aid in visual tracking. Use material with less print on the page. Consider the size of the print on the page.
Improper eye movements. Unable to keep the place.	Visual defects. Poor coordination of the eyes. Head movement. Nervousness. Meager vocabulary. Excessive articulation. Insufficient eye-span work. Pointing to the words. Word-by-word reading.	Correct physical defects if possible. Reduce head and body movement. Encourage the pupil to move the eyes rather than the head. Consider the number of words and the size of the print on the page. Develop a large, automatically recognized sight vocabulary. Use a marker, if needed, to aid in visual tracking.
Mispronunciations	Auditory perception weakness. Speech impediment. Overdependence on context clues. Carelessness. Material too difficult. Poor teaching.	Apply word attack methods at the level where skill weaknesses are noted. Flash cards/tachistoscope. Build a large vocabulary.
Narrow span of automatic word recognition	Visual defects. Not enough eye-span work. Limited meaning vocabulary. Pupil using phonics on sight words. Materials too difficult. Poor teaching.	Correct visual defects. Use matched materials. Repeated Readings/tachistoscope. Less emphasis on phonics. Much eye-span work—phrase reading. Increase meaning vocabulary.

Small meaning vocabulary	Lack of experience. Small speaking vocabulary. Lack of "languaging" at home.	Systematic vocabulary instruction. Semantic mapping. Films/film-strips. Develop the use of context. Work on structural analysis. Familiarity with dictionary.
Failure to differentiate words somewhat different in spelling	Lack of attention to meaning. Low mental abilities. Visual defects. Carelessness. Short recognition span. Inaccurate perception.	Context work—use Maze procedure. Correct physical defects, if possible.
Inaccuracy in reading passages	Carelessness. Visual defects. Too much pressure. Nervousness. Reading too fast. Low mental abilities. Materials too difficult. Material uninteresting. Defective beginning methods.	Try behavior modification techniques. Check closely on material read and keep daily record of all errors made. Use interesting material that is not too difficult. Give written directions requiring exact reading (recipes...). Accept only accurate interpretation. Correct physical defects, if possible.
Failure to note small words or key words carefully	Visual defects. Carelessness. Reads too fast. Context reader. Lack of proficient sight word recognition.	Correct visual defects, if possible. Give material that requires exact, close reading. Keep a record of daily errors so that pupil may be able to see progress made. Develop a sight vocabulary where words are practiced to the automatic level.
Repetitions	Visual problems. Material too difficult. Inadequate sight/meaning vocabulary. Insufficient phrase drill. Poor use of context.	Correct visual defects, if possible. Interesting, attractive material on the pupil's Instructional Level. Drop to the Independent Level, if necessary, to break this pattern of reading. Develop a good sight vocabulary. Eye-span work. Silent reading of material preceding oral reading.
Substitutions or insertions that change the meaning of the content	Visual defects. Limited sight vocabulary. Lack of context use while reading.	Read silently, for a purpose, and discuss before reading orally. Attend to problem of words before reading. Give written directions to be carried out. Correct vision.
Substitutions or insertions with no significant change in meaning	Eyes travel faster than the voice. Depends too much on context.	Not so much oral reading. Ask questions which require re-reading and use of exact words.
Omissions of portions of reading selection	Visual defects. Visual tracking problems. Reading too fast. Nervousness. Inattention.	Correct visual defects, if possible. Read silently and discuss before reading aloud. Reduce pressure on the pupil. Select material on the pupil's Instructional or Independent Levels. Build an adequate sight vocabulary.

Improper phrasing in sentences	Lack of training in use of context. Dialect/language differences. Lack of training in the use of context. Moving beyond the reader's instructional level. Inability to recognize thought units. Short eye-span. Inattention to punctuation marks in a sentence. Spoken vocabulary may be limited.	Instruction in the use of context. ESL placement for the second language pupil. Work on context again (Boy! I think I'm suffering from typing disability!!). Instruction at Instructional Level providing for sufficient mastery before moving to the next level of materials.
Unable to relay orally the content of material just read	Material too difficult. Not interested in the reading material. Lack of automatic word recognition abilities. Failure of the teacher to set a purpose for reading.	Use a directed reading approach (e.g., DRA, DRTA, or SQ3R), setting a purpose for reading. Use interesting materials suited to the pupil's ability. Work on sight vocabulary.
Unable to answer questions on material read	Material too difficult. Pupil's background inadequate for understanding what was read. Reading without a purpose. Failure to direct attention to meaning.	Use material at the pupil's Instructional Level. Drop to Independent, if needed. Use a directed reading approach. Use QAR. Use small unites at first, perhaps a sentence or phrase. Gradually increase the amount to be read.
Reversals in reading	Visual defects. Visual perception difficulties. Unable to attack new words. Reading material too difficult.	Correct visual defects. Use a kinesthetic method (VAKT) on letters and words. Teach left to right sequence of sounds in words. Provide materials at the appropriate level.
Unable to find the main idea, locate information, use table of contents, use an index, follow directions, make an outline, use the encyclopedia, use maps, use globes, or read charts.	Training may not have been provided. Lack of sufficient practice to master the skill. Skill instruction may have been presented to the pupil too soon. Teacher may have assumed that the pupil has received sufficient instruction at an earlier grade level. Child has Norwegian parents.	Provide instruction suited to the ability of the pupil. Provide sufficient practice to master the skill. Evaluate performance periodically and re-teach when necessary. Systematically reduce the pupil's consumption of lutefisk. Lefse is, okay.

Chapter Six

Assessment in Reading

To demonstrate that one's performance on standardized tests is determined by culture and experience, I developed this assessment instrument for use with my undergraduate education students at Eastern Washington University.

The Alaska Mental Abilities Test

1. The capital of Alaska is:

   A. Juneau
   B. Anchorage
   C. Fairbanks
   D. Nome
   E. Oil

2. A "cheechako" is:

   A. A slime ball
   B. A newcomer
   C. An oldcomer
   D. A type of salmon
   E. The sound of a sneeze at 50 below

3. A "sourdough" is:

   A. A bum
   B. An oldtimer in Alaska
   C. A native of Alaska
   D. A type of French bread served in Juneau
   E. Bad money

4. Tundra means:

   A. Swampland
   B. Vast expanses of lichens and few trees
   C. Forestland in southeast Alaska
   D. Territory occupied by the Tlingit Indians
   E. ...an Inupiat word meaning "The place where your mother-in-law waits with a frozen salmon in one hand and a 30.06 in the other"

5. Muskeg means:

   A. Where you get Hudson's Bay Tea
   B. A mammal native to the Pribilof Islands
   C. Permafrost in Ketchikan
   D. A miniature moose
   E. A container for *Musbeer*

6. "Outside" means:

   A. Where your bathroom is
   B. The opposite of "inside"
   C. Not in Alaska
   D. The exterior of your house
   E. That place which is cold in January

7. "Termination Dust" means:

   A. What occurs when the Matanuska wind blows
   B. Just a few years ago, what was left on your car after traveling the Alaska highway
   C. The end of "breakup"
   D. Snow on the hills/mountains
   E. What's left of Sam McGee

8. The Sleeping Lady is:

   A. Mt. Susitna
   B. A woman spending too much time at Chilkoot Charlie's/Red Dog Saloon/Salty Dog/Malamute Saloon
   C. Better than a Pixie Spoon
   D. The result of a Spenard Divorce
   E. Your wife's reaction to sunup at 11:00 AM and sundown at 11:30 AM

9. A Spenard Divorce involves:

   A. Your spouse, an auger, and the Chena River
   B. A pistol, bullets, and Anchorage
   C. A moose and a car
   D. Juneau what I mean
   E. A gift certificate good for one treatment by Jack Kevorkian

10. "Breakup" means:

    A. The same as a Spenard Divorce
    B. What you and your spouse do each February
    C. Thawing, yourself included
    D. When your truck hits a moose
    E. Where the Glenn and Parks highways intersect

11. Kake is:

    A. The Alaskan spelling of Cake
    B. A town north of Barrow
    C. Klinkit country
    D. Tlingit country
    E. Located south of the Queen Charlotte Islands in Alaska

12. "Freeze-up" entails:

    A. Living in Fairbanks
    B. What your car does every morning
    C. The solidification of ground and water
    D. What occurs when you meet a Grizzly on a trail to your fishing hole
    E. What occurs when you meet your mother-in-law in front of "The Great Alaska Bush Company"

13. The Matanuska wind is:

    A. A gentle summer breeze
    B. "Wind" caused by cabbage gas
    C. What will make you leave the Valley
    D. A politician from Palmer
    E. A new line dance

14. The Arctic Circle is:

    A. Fine dining in too many Alaska towns
    B. Just south of Juneau
    C. A component of a new handwriting program in Kotzebue
    D. Somewhere up (t)here*
    E. Made by expert cigar smokers in freezing temperatures

15. Unalaska is:

    A. Totally not Alaskan
    B. A suburb of Dutch Harbor
    C. A big tundrated rock
    D. North of Barrow (lots of places are, ya know)
    E. Near Wasilla

16. "Rain" means:

    A. Ketchikan
    B. Ketchikan
    C. Ketchikan
    D. Ketchikan
    E. ...

17. "Haul Road" means:

    A. Where you speed (most Alaska roads!)
    B. The road upon which one hauls one's moose in the fall
    C. The road paralleling the pipeline
    D. A log truck road in the Tongass
    E. What used to be called the Al-Can

18. Nome is:

    A. A place where one used to be able to mine gold on your beach front home
    B. A diminutive gnarled fictional character
    C. North of Barrow...
    D. There is no place like _____
    E. It's not necessarily "nowhere," but you can see it from there

19. Chicken is:

    A. Afraid of Colonel Sanders
    B. Less tasty than spruce hens
    C. A town near Eagle
    D. A Fairbanks rock group
    E. North of, well, never mind ...

20. Yukon is:

    A. What a British teacher tells a discouraged child
    B. A truck
    C. A suburb of British Columbia
    D. A state in Canada
    E. A big, long river

Answer Key

1. A or E
2. B
3. B
4. B
5. A
6. C
7. D
8. A
9. B
10. C
11. D
12. C
13. C
14. D
15. C
16. E
17. C
18. A
19. C
20. A or B

Anything less than a score of 15 means placement in a resource room.

Standardized Testing in Reading

So where's the beef?:

1. Current tests tend to reflect a "bottom-up" position (heh, heh!) in reading instruction. There is a heavy reliance upon "skills" not strategies.

2. Standardized tests use very short passages (100 to 400 words) to assess comprehension abilities.

3. Uses mainly literal recall questions to test comprehension.

4. Does not assess what the student knows about the reading process.

5. Does not assess the students' motivation to read the passages, or how well they felt they read it.

6. Does not recognize that the readers' performance is influenced by prior knowledge about the subject of the passage.

7. Is subject to luck: Multiple-choice format.

8. Does not consider how a child is feeling on the day of testing.

9. Causes young children to cry!

10. Promotes the "Lake Wobegon Effect": "Where women are strong, the men are good looking, and all the children are above average." John Pikulski (1989) reported a survey conducted by a West Virginia Physician. He found that 82% of 3,503 school districts and 100% of the 32 states surveyed with mandated testing programs reported that the average score for students in that district or state was "above average." Consider, as well, the following: We know that the variable that accounts for the most variance in standardized test scores is socioeconomic status.

"The amount of skill instruction in elementary school reading programs is excessive and absurd. Learning to read for many children is made proportionately more difficult with every added skill. Children do not learn to read fluently by learning a set of prescribed and protracted skills. Children learn to read fluently by reading. The only reason I can conjecture—and it is a completely misguided one—for the amount of reading skill instruction is the existence of standardized tests to measure them. And that is a classic case of the tail wagging not only the dog but, indeed, the entire kennel." (Manning, J.C. (1995). "Ariston metron." *The Reading Teacher, 48,* 650-659.)

Assumptions about Portfolios

- Portfolios are systematic, purposeful, and meaningful collections of students' works in one or more subject areas.

- Students of any age or grade level can learn not only to select pieces to be placed into their portfolios but can also learn to establish criteria for their selections.

- Portfolio collections may include input by teachers, parents, peers, and school administrators.

- In all cases, portfolios should reflect the actual day-to-day learning activities of students.

- Portfolios should be ongoing so that they show the students' efforts, progress, and achievements over a period of time.

- Portfolios may contain several compartments, or subfolders.

- Selected works in portfolios may be in a variety of media and may be multidimensional.

Checklist for Providing a Balanced Focus in Reading/Writing Instruction

Are students being given opportunities to develop positive attitudes toward reading?

    Are you providing for daily Sustained Silent Reading?

    In reading, are you encouraging students to immerse themselves in reading and responding?

    Do you provide ample opportunity to discuss interesting ideas from books and writing?

    Are students encouraged to share what they have reading? What they have written?

    Do you provide guidance in selecting good books. and support in reading them?

    What other practices promote a positive view of reading and writing?

Are students directed toward important content in their reading and writing?

    Are you providing support for students to identify the important information in text?

    Are questions focused on important information in text?

    Are students expected to integrate information from a variety of sources?

Do students have ample opportunity to acquire important process skills?

    Do you provide direct instruction in reading strategies and processes?

    Do you model effective reading strategies for students?

    Do you help students to acquire important information about reading?

    Are students encouraged to recognize patterns in their reading so that they can use the knowledge and skill they possess?